Carolyn Pressler
The View of Women Found in the
Deuteronomic Family Laws

# Beihefte zur Zeitschrift für die alttestamentliche Wissenschaft

Herausgegeben von
Otto Kaiser

Band 216

Walter de Gruyter · Berlin · New York
1993

Carolyn Pressler

# The View of Women Found in the Deuteronomic Family Laws

Walter de Gruyter · Berlin · New York

1993

∞ Printed on acid-free paper which falls
within the guidelines of the ANSI to ensure
permanence and durability

*Library of Congress Cataloging-in-Publication Data*

Pressler, Carolyn, 1952—
  The view of women found in the Deuteronomic family laws /
Carolyn Pressler.
        p.    cm. — (Beihefte zur Zeitschrift für die alttestament-
liche Wissenschaft ; Bd. 216)
  Revision of a Ph.D. thesis submitted to Princeton Theological
Seminary, 1991.
  Includes bibliographical references.
  ISBN 3-11-013743-7 (alk. paper) : $ 76.00
  1. Bible. O.T. Deuteronomy—Criticism, interpretation, etc.    2. Wo-
men in the Bible.    3. Jewish law—Sources.    4. Women—Legal
status, laws, etc. (Jewish law)    I. Title.    II. Series: Beihefte zur
Zeitschrift für die alttestamentliche Wissenschaft ; 216.
BS410.Z5    vol. 216
[BS1275.6.W7]
222′ . 15083054—dc20                                          93-27800
                                                                    CIP

*Die Deutsche Bibliothek — Cataloging in Publication Data*

**Pressler, Carolyn:** The view of women found in the Deuteronomic
family laws / Carolyn Pressler. — Berlin ; New York : de Gruyter,
1993
    (Beihefte zur Zeitschrift für die alttestamentliche Wissenschaft ;
    Bd. 216)
    Zugl.: Princeton, Univ., Diss., 1991
    ISBN 3-11-013743-7
NE: Zeitschrift für die alttestamentliche Wissenschaft / Beihefte

ISSN 0934-2575

Printed in Germany
Printing: Arthur Collignon GmbH, Berlin
Binding: Lüderitz & Bauer-GmbH, Berlin

# Acknowledgments

I wish to thank Prof. Dr. Otto Kaiser, the editor of *BZAW*, and the publishers Walter de Gruyter and Co. for accepting my manuscript for publication in this series.

This monograph is a revision of a thesis by the same title submitted to Princeton Theological Seminary for the degree of Ph.D. in 1991. I wish to express heartfelt thanks to my thesis adviser, Katharine Doob Sakenfeld, for her rigorous, responsive, and compassionate counsel and for her continued friendship. I am also deeply grateful to my readers, Dr. Patrick Miller and Dr. Dennis Olson for their extensive feedback and ongoing support.

My colleagues at United Theological Seminary of the Twin Cities have assisted with this project in numerous ways. I am especially thankful to Dean Wilson Yates for providing me with the reduced course load, research assistants, and encouragement necessary to finish the manuscript, and to Prof. Arthur Merrill for his insights and encouragement. I also wish to thank Janis Best, Carol Shaffer and Susan Ebbers, who proofread and edited the monograph.

The manuscript was made camera-ready by Dr. Richard Whitaker. I am indebted to him for that work as well as for hours of conversation about Deuteronomic law.

# Contents

# Abbreviations

| | |
|---|---|
| AHML | E. Neufeld, *Ancient Hebrew Marriage Laws* |
| AICL | A. Phillips, *Ancient Israel's Criminal Law: A New Approach to the Decalogue* |
| AL | *The Assyrian Laws*, Ed. G. R. Driver, J. C. Miles |
| ANET | *Ancient Near Eastern Texts Relating to the Old Testament*, Ed. J. B. Pritchard |
| AOAT | *Alter Orient und Altes Testament* |
| BDB | F. Brown, S. R. Driver, and C. A. Briggs, *A Hebrew and English Lexicon of the Old Testament* |
| BMA | M. Roth, *Babylonian Marriage Agreements* |
| CBQ | *Catholic Biblical Quarterly* |
| CE | Code of Eshnunna |
| CH | Code of Hammurabi |
| DBS | *Dictionnaire de la Bible Supplément* |
| DDS | M. Weinfeld, *Deuteronomy and the Deuteronomic School* |
| GKC | *Gesenius' Hebrew Grammar*, Ed. E. Kautzsch, A. E. Cowley |
| HL | Hittite Laws |
| IDB | *Interpreter's Dictionary of the Bible* |
| IDBSup | *Interpreter's Dictionary of the Bible*, Supplementary Volume |
| JAOS | *Journal of the American Oriental Society* |
| JBL | *Journal of Biblical Literature* |
| JJS | *Journal of Jewish Studies* |
| JLA | *Jewish Law Annual* |
| JNES | *Journal of Near Eastern Studies* |
| JSOT | *Journal for the Study of the Old Testament* |
| LXX | Septuagint |
| MAL | Middle Assyrian Laws |
| MT | Masoretic text |
| NBL | Neo-Babylonian Laws |
| NRSV | New Revised Standard Version |
| OBML | R. Westbrook, "Old Babylonian Marriage Law" |
| OT | Old Testament |
| RIDA | *Revue Internationale des Droits de l'Antiquité* |
| SamP | Samaritan Pentateuch |
| SBCL | R. Westbrook, *Studies in Biblical and Cuneiform Law* |
| TDOT | *Theological Dictionary of the Old Testament* |
| VT | *Vetus Testamentum* |
| ZAW | *Zeitschrift für die alttestamentliche Wissenschaft* |

# Introduction

The purpose of this study is to examine the view of women found within the Deuteronomic family laws. Several recent discussions have suggested that these laws manifest a highly positive appraisal of women's status.[1] In contrast, we will argue that the laws presuppose the dependence of women within male-headed households and the subordinate role of women within the family. The laws aim to support the stability of the family by undergirding hierarchical, patrilineal family structures. They also protect dependent family members. Their efforts to protect dependents do not, however, fundamentally challenge the hierarchical family structure.

The position of this study is more consistent with findings of earlier studies by Roland de Vaux and Johannes Pedersen which argue that Israelite women held a dependent status within a thoroughly patriarchal family.[2] These early studies, however, fail to differentiate between texts from different historical periods, geographical areas, or social spheres in their discussion of women. Thus, they shed little light on the particular concerns of Deuteronomic family law as that law relates to women.[3]

## 1. *The Scope of the Study*

This study is limited to the view of the status of women within the family found within four sets of laws:
1. Deut 21:10-21 -- the law of the captive bride; the law of primogeniture; the law of the rebellious son;
2. Deut 22:13-29 -- sexual offense laws;
3. Deut 24:1-4 -- the prohibition of the restoration of marriage; and
4. Deut 25:5-12 -- the law of levirate marriage and the law of breach of modesty.

Deuteronomic law shows no concern for the status of women per se. Rather, women come into view in laws having other concerns. These laws fall into several categories. References to women as widows are found in a set of laws which protect vulnerable landless people.[4] The

---

1    See below, pp. 5-6.
2    Roland de Vaux, *Ancient Israel: Its Life and Institutions*, (New York: McGraw-Hill, 1961), 19-40; Johannes Pedersen, *Israel: Its Life and Culture*, vol. 1 (London: Oxford University Press, 1926), 46-81.
3    Methodological problems in de Vaux's and Pedersen's studies will be discussed in more detail below, pp. 6-7.
4    Deut 16:11, 14; 24:17, 19, 20, 21; 26:12-13; see also 10:18 and 27:19. Concern for the fatherless and the unsupported widow (הַיָּתוֹם וְהָאַלְמָנָה) is a common topos not only

Deuteronomic war laws refer to captured women as potential spoil and to betrothal as a reason for exemption from military service.[5] Women are also found in laws having to do with slavery[6] and with purity.[7] Finally, women are found in laws having to do with family relationships.

Discussions of the Deuteronomic view of women are distortive when they fail to take into consideration the categories of laws in which the references to women are found and the roles played by the women discussed in those laws. One scholar, for example, cites Deuteronomic laws protecting widows as evidence of Deuteronomic concern for women.[8] Given the association of "widow," "fatherless," and "resident alien" in Deuteronomy and throughout the ancient Near East, these laws should be taken as evidence of Deuteronomic concern for the poor, not for women as such. Similarly, the fact that Deut 15:12-18 grants release to female as well as male indentured servants must be understood in relationship to other slave laws. Both in biblical law and in the cuneiform codes, slave laws explicitly refer to males and females, and consistently treat both sexes alike unless they concern matters of sexuality or reproduction. Unlike its parallel in Ex 21:7-11, the Deuteronomic law of release is not specifically concerned with the female slave's sexuality. She is not a concubine. The reference to the female slave in the Deuteronomic law of release is exactly what one would expect.[9]

Thus, it is necessary for methodological reasons for a discussion of references to women in these laws to take account of the particular roles

---

in Deuteronomy, but throughout the ancient Near East. Harriet Katherine Havice, "The Concern for the Widow and the Fatherless in the Ancient Near East: A Case Study in Old Testament Ethics," (Ph.D. diss., Yale University, 1978) has studied the tradition history of prohibitions against maltreatment of these vulnerable persons.

5    Deut 20:7, 14; 24:5. The war laws include all of chap. 20; 23:10-15 (Eng. 23:9-14); 24:5. As is discussed below, the law of the captive bride, Deut 21:10-14, has affinities with both the war laws and the family laws.

6    Deut 15:12-18.

7    Deut 22:5; 23:18-19 (Eng. 23:17-18). Women are also referred to in cultic regulations. They are found in the roles of daughters and maid servants in the cultic command to "rejoice before the LORD your God" (Deut 12:12; 16:11, 14), and as wives and daughters in the law concerning conspiracy to commit apostasy (Deut 13:7-12 [Eng. 13:6-11]). These last do not appear to belong to a homogeneous category, however.

8    Pierre Rémy, "La Condition de la femme dans les codes du Proche-Orient ancien et les codes d'Israel," *Sciences Ecclesiastiques* 16 (1964): 298.

9    Scholars frequently contrast Deut 15:12, which explicitly states that the law of release applies to females and to males, with Ex 21:7, which explicitly states that the law of release does not apply to the אָמָה, the handmaiden. The contrast is supposed to illustrate Deuteronomy's humane view of women. See Moshe Weinfeld, *Deuteronomy and the Deuteronomic School* (Oxford: Clarendon Press, 1972), 282. The Exodus law, however, has to do with a young woman purchased for concubinage; the Deuteronomic law does not. That difference in the two cases explains why the Exodus law and the Deuteronomic law treat the woman differently.

played by the women and of the kind of laws in which the references are found.[10]

This study will focus on the status of women found within laws whose primary concern is the family.[11] Each of the laws listed above treats aspects of the relationship between a man and his wife, and/or aspects of the relationship between parents and their offspring.[12]

---

10    Ideally, one would examine the status of women suggested by each of the various categories of Deuteronomic laws, as well as the exclusion or inclusion of women in other spheres of life addressed by Deuteronomic law (e.g., in the assembly of Yahweh, chap. 23). One would also inquire whether and when women were included among audiences addressed by the laws, and when and whether women's behavior was a concern of the laws. Such a study is beyond the scope of this work.

11    Alexander Rofé, "Family and Sex Laws in Deuteronomy and the Book of the Covenant," *Henoch* 9, 2 (1987): 131-160; Patrick D. Miller, *Deuteronomy*, Interpretation: A Biblical Commentary for Teaching and Preaching (Louisville: John Knox Press, 1990), 163-169; Naomi Steinberg, "Adam's and Eve's Daughters are Many," (Ph.D. diss., Columbia University, 1984); and Weinfeld, *DDS*, treat Deuteronomic family legislation. My categorization differs from theirs in that I include Deut 21:10-14, the law of the captive bride, with the family laws. The law is indeed connected to the war laws by its opening phrase, כִּי־תֵצֵא לַמִּלְחָמָה, "when you go out to battle," which is also found in Deut 20:1, and its reference to captives. The primary concerns of Deut 21:10-14, however, are marriage and the termination of marriage; the law thus has to do with the family as much or more than it has to do with war. Moreover, the law of the captive bride is associated with the other family laws by overlapping vocabulary and by placement (see pp. 4-5).

    Two laws, Deut 23:1 (Eng. 22:29) and 24:5 might have been included in this study of family laws but were not. The content of Deut 23:1 (which prohibits sexual relationships between a man and his father's wives) has to do with family relationships. The form of the law, however, sets it apart from the other Deuteronomic family laws. Deut 23:1 is apodictic; the family laws examined in this study are casuistic in form. Because of this, commentators are widely agreed that Deut 23:1 is a late addition to these laws. Deut 24:5, which exempts a newly married man from military or other service to the state has affinities to the family laws. It is more closely tied, however, to the military exemptions in Deut 20:5-7 which include the exemption of any man who has betrothed but not married a woman. Therefore, this study has followed Alexander Rofé, "The Laws of Warfare in the Book of Deuteronomy: Their Origins, Intent and Positivity," *JSOT* 32 (1985): 23-44; Miller, *Deuteronomy*, 156; and most commentators in classifying Deut 24:5 with the war laws.

12    Aspects of the marriage relationship are the concern of 21:10-13, which provides a legal way for a man to marry a captive woman; 21:14, which prohibits that man from selling the woman; 22:13-29, a series of laws which together treat adultery; 24:1-4, which prohibits remarriage under certain circumstances; 25:5-10, which promotes levirate marriage, and 25:11-12, which penalizes a married woman's breach of modesty. Parent-child relationships are the focus of Deut 21:15-17, which protects the rights of a chronologically first-born son; Deut 21:18-21, which prescribes capital punishment for a rebellious son, and Deut 22:20-21, which demands the death penalty for a licentious bride/daughter.

## 2. The Interconnectedness of the Deuteronomic Family Laws

The texts examined in this study were selected primarily because they deal with a common topic: family relationships. The interconnectedness of these laws is also suggested by associations discernible within the laws such as vocabulary, structure, and, to some extent, placement. This interconnectedness in turn suggests that we may expect some consistency in the viewpoint of these laws concerning women's status within the family.

The interconnectedness of the laws is suggested by distinctive phrases and vocabulary. Similar motive clauses are found in Deut 21:14 (the law of the captive bride) and 22:28-29 (the last of the laws which define adultery). In 21:14, a man is prohibited from selling his captive bride, because he has had his way with her, תַּחַת אֲשֶׁר עִנִּיתָהּ. In 22:29, a man must marry a young woman whom he has violated, and is prohibited from ever divorcing her for the same reason, תַּחַת אֲשֶׁר עִנָּהּ. Deut 24:1-4 (the prohibition against the restoration of marriage) is linked to Deut 22:13-29 (laws concerning adultery) by the same beginning phrase: כִּי־יִקַּח אִישׁ אִשָּׁה "if a man takes a wife." Phrases such as "to take" or "to give a wife," (Deut 21:10-14; 22:13-19; 24:1-4; 25:5-10), and words like "father," "mother," "son," and "daughter" (Deut 21:15-17, 18-21; 22:13-21; 25:5-10) are perhaps too common to consider as deliberate links between the laws. The presence of this vocabulary in the family laws may be explained by their content. Other terms repeated within the different laws are less common. The term בְּכוֹר, "first-born son," forms a link between 21:15-17 and 25:5-10. The verb בעל, used in the sense of "to marry," (Deut 21:13, 24:1, and 22:22) and the *piel* stem of שׁלח, meaning "to divorce," (Deut 22:19, 29; 24:1, 3, 4) are relatively rare in the Hebrew Bible. Their use in the laws under examination draws further connections between those texts.

A distinctive structure is found in three of the cases. Deut 21:18-21 (the law of the rebellious son), Deut 22:13-19 (the law of the slandered bride) and Deut 25:7-10 (the second part of the law of levirate marriage) are set at the gate, before the elders. In each of the cases, a legal introduction is followed by a description of the case, then by an instruction to the plaintiff to come before the elders and state the charge. In each case, the words of the charge closely reflect the language of the description of the case. The instructions are followed by the statement of penalty. This structure is not found anywhere else in biblical law; it further signals the interconnectedness of the Deuteronomic family laws.

Finally, several of the laws are associated with each other by their placement within the book of Deuteronomy. The law of the captured bride, the law of primogeniture, and the law of the rebellious son are located together (21:10-21). The adultery laws of Deut 22:13-29 are grouped together, as are the law of levirate marriage and the law concerning breach of modesty (Deut 25:5-12). Further associations discernible among these laws will be explored in the exegetical discussion in part 1 (chapters 1-4).

## 3. *Review of the Literature*

This study will argue that the Deuteronomic family laws presuppose and undergird male headed and male defined hierarchical family structures, in which women hold subordinate and dependent statuses. In one sense, such a position is not unexpected; the patriarchal character of Israelite society has been widely recognized. This position is in sharp contrast, however, to recent scholarly discussions of the Deuteronomic view of women. Moshe Weinfeld holds that the Deuteronomic laws exhibit a peculiarly humane attitude toward women; the Deuteronomic redactors are supposed to have espoused the "equality of the sexes."[13] Naomi Steinberg believes that Deuteronomic family legislation demonstrates the non-hierarchical character of relationships between women and men in the Israelite family.[14] Pierre Rémy and John Goldingay also believe that Deuteronomic law is especially concerned with women,[15] while Anthony Phillips and David Daube argue that this was the first Israelite law to treat women as legal persons.[16]

Three methodological problems bring these scholars' conclusions into question. First, all of the recent considerations of the Deuteronomic view of women have assumed that the legal aims of the family legislation are self-evident. Often their claims that a law supports or protects women are made without offering an exegetical basis for these claims. The purpose of each of the family laws is debatable; each must be subjected to thoroughgoing exegetical study before its presuppositions and purposes regarding women can be analyzed.

Second, study of the Deuteronomic view of women's status within the family must take into consideration the familial and societal patterns presupposed by the laws, as well as their aim or purpose. Laws aimed at protecting women in given situations may be necessary precisely because

---

13   Weinfeld, *DDS*, 291.
14   Steinberg, "Adam's and Eve's Daughters," 275 and 279.
15   Rémy, "La Condition de la femme," 296-299; John Goldingay, *Theological Diversity and the Authority of the Old Testament* (Grand Rapids: Eerdmans, 1987), 138.
16   Anthony Phillips, *Ancient Israel's Criminal Law: A New Approach to the Decalogue* (Oxford: Basil Blackwell, 1970), 180; David Daube, "Biblical Landmarks in the Struggle for Women's Rights," *Juridical Review* 23, 3 (1978): 177-180. These scholars' discussions are brief. The longest treatment is Steinberg's chapter-length analysis of the status of women within the Israelite family suggested by the family laws in Deut 19-25 (Steinberg, "Adam's and Eve's Daughters," 240-272).

the woman is seen as particularly dependent and vulnerable. For
example, Deut 22:28-29 requires a man who rapes an unbetrothed virgin
to marry her, and prohibits him from ever divorcing her. An aim of the
law is to protect the woman. The presuppositions of the law, however,
indicate the woman's unchallenged subordinate status: (1) women are
dependent upon male-headed households for security and social status;
(2) the marriageability of a woman is defined in terms of her virginity; (3)
men normally were able to divorce their wives easily (otherwise, the
prohibition against divorce would be a meaningless penalty); and (4) as
comparison of this law with Deut 22:22-27 and Ex 22:15-16 (Eng.
22:16-17) suggests, the woman's consent or lack of consent to sexual
intercourse was a negligible factor in determining the gravity of a sexual
offense. Clearly, it is not enough to examine only the purpose of the laws.
One must also consider the presuppositions of the laws concerning
women's status within the family.

Third, with the exception of Steinberg, these scholars discuss women
in the abstract, apart from the family context. They therefore pay
attention to aspects of the laws which protect dependent family members,
but disregard aspects of the laws which serve the interest of the male
head of household or suppport hierarchical structures of family authority.
Their assessment of the view of women found in the Deuteronomic family
laws is, consequently, one-sided.

Steinberg rightly argues that women and men must be studied in
relationship to one another and in the context of the family. This allows
her to identify areas of interdependence between women and men, to
examine the multiple interests served by a given law, and to conceptualize
Israelite women as actors as well as objects. Steinberg exaggerates the
degree to which the Deuteronomic family laws treat women and men
symmetrically, however, and she simply disregards asymmetrical
responses to women and men in them.[17] What is needed is a careful
examination of the family patterns relating to women presupposed or
supported by the laws, taking into account both gender symmetry and
asymmetry.

The broad outlines of the position of this study are consistent with
conclusions drawn by earlier scholars. De Vaux and Pedersen both argue
that Israelite women held subordinate statuses within a patriarchal
family. De Vaux points to terminology used to denote the husband, *ba'al*

---

17    Steinberg, "Adam's and Eve's Daughters," 251-254. For example, she wrongly claims
      that Deut 22:13-21 requires that both the slanderous husband and the unchaste bride
      be put to death for perjuring themselves. In fact, Deut 22:19 prescribes a fine for the
      slanderous husband while Deut 22:20-21 demands the death penalty for the unchaste
      bride. Steinberg also disregards the asymmetrical treatment of women and men
      found in the Deuteronomic adultery laws, laws which require fidelity of a married
      woman but not of a married man.

(master), *'adon* (lord), as evidence of his dominant status. He enumerates women's unequal rights in legal matters such as inheritance and divorce. He also correctly notes that the Old Testament does not treat women as slaves or as mere possessions. The laws protect women and the narratives suggest women's capacity to participate in public affairs.[18] Pedersen develops a very similar portrait of Israelite women's status. He argues that Israelite men exercised dominance but not a wholly one-sided sovereignty. Male-female relationships were characterized by intimacy as well as by authority. Pedersen also points out the one-sidedness of biblical marriage and divorce laws, and highlights the biblical emphasis on childbearing.[19]

Further study is likely to bear out the broad outlines of de Vaux's and Pedersen's positions; it is less likely to support the details of their analyses. Both scholars indiscriminately draw on texts from widely varying geographical locations, social circles, and historical periods to develop composite pictures of the status of women in the Israelite family. They falsely assume that Israelite women's statuses and roles were unchanging throughout Israel's history. Bernard Batto's critique of composite pictures of women in the ancient Near East is applicable to de Vaux's and Pedersen's studies: "Mosaics constructed out of information collected from widely differing locales and times may yield neat and detailed scenes, but their accuracy is necessarily distorted by the juxtaposition of such disparate elements."[20] De Vaux and Pedersen also fail to discriminate between the pictures found in the biblical texts and ancient Israelite practice.

In the decades since these studies were published, there has been a growing recognition of the need to examine smaller and more carefully defined groups of texts. The possibility that women's statuses might have varied over time, geographical areas, and differing social and religious spheres is recognized. Recent scholarship also acknowledges the difference between text and social practice, and especially between ideal

---

18   de Vaux, *Ancient Israel*, 19-40.

19   Pedersen, *Israel*, 46-81. Pedersen provides no exegetical basis for his interpretation of the "psychic community" which shaped the family and which bore the father's stamp. This aspect of his discussion is overly romantic.

20   Bernard Frank Batto, *Studies on Women at Mari* (Baltimore: Johns Hopkins University Press, 1974), 4.

Such "distortion of accuracy" is apparent in de Vaux's assumption that daughters whose fathers had no sons could inherit their fathers' property throughout Israel's history (*Ancient Israel*, 54). It is seen in Pedersen's treatment of slave wives. Pedersen juxtaposes a range of legal and narrative material that may have to do with slave wives; he assumes that the captive bride (Deut 21:10-14) is such a slave wife (*Israel*, 72-74). Pedersen also interprets Num 30 in light of his composite picture (*Israel*, 70). Since that picture places great emphasis on progeny, he interprets the wife's vows which a husband might veto as vows of sexual abstinence.

law and actual judicial decisions.[21] This study will focus on a narrow set of texts, the Deuteronomic family laws, which reflect the values of a relatively homogeneous group of redactors. It will acknowledge that the Deuteronomic ideals may or may not correspond to actual Israelite legal or social practice.

In contrast to recent discussions of the view of women found in Deuteronomic law, especially Deuteronomic family law, this study will begin with a thorough exegetical study of each of the sets of family legislation (chapters 1-4). It will then analyze both the family patterns related to women which are presupposed by the laws (chapter 5) and the overall purposes of the Deuteronomic family laws as those purposes relate to women (chapter 6).

---

21   Recently published bibliographies demonstrate the more narrow and controlled focus of recent studies of Israelite women, or of the Bible and women. See esp. Peggy L. Day, ed., *Gender and Difference in Ancient Israel* (Minneapolis: Fortress Press, 1989), 199-202.

# PART ONE: Exegesis

## Chapter One: Relationships of Authority Within the Family: Deuteronomy 21:10-21

### 1. *Introduction*

The three laws found in Deut 21:10-21 are grouped around a common concern for the family. That is, they define relationships of authority between heads of households and their dependents. Deut 21:10-14, the law of the captive bride, and Deut 21:15-17, the law of primogeniture, define the rights of two kinds of dependent family members: a captive woman made wife and a chronologically first-born son. They do so by first assuming and then limiting the authority of the husband or father. The third law, Deut 21:18-21, the law of the rebellious son, resolutely asserts the authority of the father and mother over their offspring. The three laws taken together thus express a concern for a hierarchical structure of authority within the family and a concern for the status and rights of dependent family members.

### 2. *The Captive Bride: Deuteronomy 21:10-14*

Deut 21:10-14 belongs to a group of Deuteronomic laws concerning warfare.[1] The introduction of the law, כִּי־תֵצֵא לַמִּלְחָמָה, refers explicitly to battle, and ties the law firmly to chapter 20, a compendium of war laws which begins with precisely the same phrase. Deut 21:10-14 is also linked to the other war laws by similarity of content, in that it concerns warriors and captives, and by similarity of form, in that most of the war laws take the "if-you" form.

Deut 21:10-14 belongs equally to the Deuteronomic family laws, however.[2] It is connected to them by content, in that it concerns marriage and divorce. The motive clause found in v. 14, תַּחַת אֲשֶׁר עִנִּיתָהּ, is found also in the law concerning the violation of an unbetrothed girl (Deut 22:29), further linking the law to other Deuteronomic family legislation. Finally, the law is followed by two family laws.

Deut 21:10-14 contains a case and a sub-case. The law contained in vv. 10-13 discusses a case where the sphere of war/foreign nations penetrates into the domestic sphere. It provides a legal way for a man to marry a foreign captive woman. The prohibition in v. 14 belongs entirely to the

---

1    Deut 20; 21:10-14; 23:10-15 (Eng. 23:9-14); and 24:5.
2    Deut 21:10-21; 22:13-29; 24:1-4; and 25:5-12.

sphere of family law; the woman has become the wife of an Israelite man, and is protected from enslavement by that status.

### a. *Deuteronomy 21:10-13*

The law set out in Deut 21:10-13 is drafted in second person singular. It directly addresses the warrior, and, in the first place, regulates his behavior. Verse 12 changes to third person feminine and concerns the behavior of the woman. The switch from direct address to third person may indicate that the warrior addressed is responsible for seeing that the woman's actions are carried out.

One's interpretation of Deut 21:10-13 depends largely on where one understands the protasis to end and the apodosis to begin. It is possible to interpret the law as if the protasis extends only through v. 11a: "When you go out to battle against your enemies and the Lord your God gives them into your hands, and you take them captive, if you see among the captives a beautiful woman and desire her." The apodosis then begins with the command "Then you shall take her as your wife, and bring her to your household." It is also possible to extend the protasis through v. 11 to the *athnah* at v. 12. The law then reads: "When you go out to battle against your enemies and the Lord your God gives them into your hands, and you take them captive, if you see among the captives a beautiful woman whom you desire and want to marry and bring into your your household, then she shall shave her head, and pare her nails."[3]

This latter translation is preferable for two reasons. First, beginning the apodosis at v. 11b creates a sequence of events which is out of order. The warrior addressed by the law is to marry the woman (וְלָקַחְתָּ לְךָ לְאִשָּׁה). Then the woman is to perform three ritual actions and mourn her parents for one month, after which the man is to go in to her and marry her (וּבְעַלְתָּהּ). The man appears to be told to marry the woman twice. The awkwardness of having the man marry the captive woman before and after her month of mourning is eliminated by extending the protasis through v. 12a. If the man wishes to marry the woman and bring her into his household, then she must perform the rituals and mourn her parents. After that he may go to her and marry her.

Second, there is a change of person at the *athnah* in v. 12. The law begins in second person, addressing the warrior who desires the woman. At the *athnah* in v. 12, it switches to third person feminine singular, and states actions that the woman is to perform. This break in syntax may well signal the break between the protasis and the apodosis.

---

3  The NRSV begins the protasis at the *athnah* of v. 12. It reads: "Suppose you see among the captives a beautiful woman whom you desire and want to marry, and so you bring her home to your house; she shall shave her head, pare her nails, discard her captive's garb, and shall remain in your house a full month, mourning for her father and mother."

We will argue that this law provides a means for the man to marry a woman in a case where the normal procedures for marriage are not possible, and provides a way for the foreign woman to be assimilated into an Israelite household.

Commentators frequently understand the purpose of this law as a prohibition against rape on the battlefield.[4] It is unlikely that this was the aim of the law. We have argued that the law should not be translated to read: "If you desire her, then you shall marry her." Rather, the man's desire to marry the woman is part of the protasis. The law has to do with a case where a man wishes to marry a foreign captive; it then provides a means for him to do so. Moreover, the law is concerned with what happens within the household, not what happens on the battlefield. All of the actions commanded by the law take place within the household. Finally, such a prohibition would not be in keeping with the tenor of Deut 20:14 which instructs the soldiers to plunder the wives and children of their enemies: "Devour the spoil of your enemies."

Rather, the law has two main purposes. The first purpose seems to be to provide a legal means for the man to marry a woman in a situation where the normal procedures for contracting a marriage are impossible. Marriage in the ancient Near East normally involved a contractual arrangement between the groom or his parents and the parents of the bride. CH 128 and CE 27 and 28 appear to state that the existence of such a contract determined whether the relationship between a man and a woman was considered a legal marriage.[5] A contractual arrangement with the woman's father, mother, brother or master appears to be constitutive of marriage in ancient Israel as well.[6] In the case of the captive woman,

---

4    Miller writes, "Rape is not a rule of war, not even humiliation of women" (*Deuteronomy*, 159). Gerhard von Rad, *Deuteronomy: A Commentary*, trans. Dorothea Barton, Old Testament Library (Philadelphia: Westminster Press, 1966), 137; Rémy, "La condition de la femme," 297; and Samuel R. Driver, *A Critical and Exegetical Commentary on Deuteronomy*, International Critical Commentary (Edinburgh: T. & T. Clark, 1902), 244, also hold this position.

5    CH 128, *ANET*, 171; CE 27, 28, *ANET*, 162. See also Reuven Yaron, *The Laws of Eshnunna*, 2d rev. ed. (Jerusalem: Magnes Press, 1988), 200-205.

6    Cf. Ex 22:15-16 (Eng. 22:16-17); Deut 22:28-29; and also Gen 34. Shechem's offense is not necessarily that he has had sexual intercourse with Dinah against her will. Rather, he has failed to acquire the consent of Dinah's father. Gen 34:2 uses three verbs to describe Shechem's offense: לקח, שכב, and ענה. None of these verbs necessarily implies forcible violation. לקח and שכב can each be used separately to refer to sexual intercourse without any suggestion of physical violence. The two verbs are found together in two other places in the Hebrew Bible: 2 Sam 11:4 and 2 Sam 12:11. In 2 Sam 11:4, David sends his messengers to fetch (לקח) Bathsheba who comes to him, whereupon he lies (שכב) with her. In 2 Sam 12:11, Nathan proclaims God's judgment against David for taking Uriah's wife, Bathsheba. God will take (לקח) David's wives and give them to another man who will lie (שכב) with them. In both cases the women's consent or lack of consent is immaterial. The verbs

such a contract is not possible.[7] The law thus provides an alternative way for the man to marry the woman.[8]

A second purpose of the law is indicated by the rituals prescribed in vv. 12-13. The former captive is to shave her head, pare her nails, and take off the garment of her captivity. She is then to mourn her father and mother for one month. It seems likely that the rituals and the mourning period serve as ways to faciliate the assimilation of the woman, a foreigner, into an Israelite household.

The precise nature and purpose of the rituals are a matter of some debate. Scholars have usually explained them either as mourning rituals[9] or as rituals marking the change in the woman's status from foreigner to Israelite.[10] The latter interpretation seems more likely for three reasons. First, the description of the ritual acts is separated from the instruction that she is to mourn her parents by the phrase "and she shall dwell in your house." The word "house" repeated in v. 12 and v. 13 forms an inclusio which frames the ritual acts and sets them apart from the mourning. The

---

taken together need not imply physical force.

The *piel* of עָנָה often is used of forcible violation, but can refer to sexual intercourse with a consenting woman (Deut 22:24, Ez 22:10). The word refers to sexual acts which are in some way improper and which debase the woman, but which do not necessarily entail force (see pp. 14-15).

Shechem's act is illicit; he has not acquired Jacob's consent. We do not know whether his act was also violent; the text does not record whether or not Dinah consented. For further discussion, see Tikva Frymer-Kensky, "Law and Philosophy: The Case of Sex in the Bible," *Semeia* 45 (1989): 100 n. 9.

7    Presumably a captive/slave would not be legally competent to enter into a contract on her own behalf.

8    The MAL include provisions for a man to marry his concubine legally by publicly veiling her (MAL A: 41, *ANET*, 183), and for a widow to enter into a common law marriage (MAL A:34, *ANET*, 183). The existence of these two laws indicates that marriages entered into without a contractual arrangement were an exception to the norm in the Middle Assyrian period and required special legal provisions. Deut 24:10-13 seems to be a similar provision for an exceptional marriage. If the *esirtu* in MAL A:41 refers to a captive woman rather than any sort of concubine (as may be indicated by the root of *esirtu*, *'sr*, "to bind"), then the law is a rather close parallel to Deut 21:10-13. It is probably best, however, to assume with Godfrey Driver and John Miles that *esirtu* has come by extension to refer to any kind of concubine. See Godfrey R. Driver and John C. Miles, *The Assyrian Laws* (Oxford: Clarendon Press, 1935), 127-128, 187.

9    von Rad, *Deuteronomy*, 137; Peter C. Craigie, *The Book of Deuteronomy*, New International Commentary on the Old Testament (Grand Rapids: Eerdmans, 1976), 281.

10   George Adam Smith, *The Book of Deuteronomy*, Cambridge Bible for Schools and Colleges (Cambridge: Cambridge University Press, 1950), 254; Anthony Phillips, *Deuteronomy*, Cambridge Bible Commentary (Cambridge: Cambridge University Press, 1973), 140; Craigie, *Deuteronomy*, 281; G. Ernest Wright, "Introduction and Exegesis," *The Book of Deuteronomy*, Interpreter's Bible (Nashville: Abingdon Press, 1953), 461.

repetition perhaps points to the reason for the rituals; a foreigner is now dwelling in the midst of the Israelite's house.

Second, putting off one's garments is not of itself a mourning ritual in the Hebrew Bible. Reference to "garments" does not in itself indicate mourning, but the fact that the garments are torn (קרע) does. To rend one's garment was a sign of mourning (Josh 7:6; Gen 44:13; Jer 41:5); to put on a new garment, a sign that mourning had ended (2 Sam 12:20). Changing or washing one's garments was a sign of purification (Gen 35:2; Ex 19:10, 14). Garments, as the object found in closest proximity to one's person, seem to symbolize one's status or even one's personality. The act of removing the "garment of captivity" should probably be understood as removing the status of captivity.

Third, while making oneself bald was indeed a mourning ritual, the verb most often used in connection with mourning is קרח. Our passage uses the verb גלח "to shave." This verb is not used in reference to shaving one's head within mourning rituals.[11] The verb is often used of shaving one's head in connection with purification rituals (Lev 14:8, 9; Num 6:9; Lev 13:33). Smith's interpretation, that the act is a purification ritual marking the entrance of a foreigner into Israel, is quite plausible.[12]

The three rituals and the period of mourning separate the woman's old life as a captive, and, prior to captivity, as a member of her parents' family, from her new life. Commentators discuss the instructions that the woman shall mourn her father and mother as expressing the lawmakers' sensitive concern for the captive's feelings. This is possibly one dimension of the law. The thirty day period between the time the man brought the captive into his house and the time he took her in marriage also served to demarcate the old from the new, and so to provide for the assimilation of a foreigner into an Israelite household.

It is not possible to say whether Deut 21:10-13 had yet a third purpose, that is, to protect the captive woman by providing her with marital status. Presumably male and female captives were brought back to serve as slaves.[13] Did the law intend to prohibit a man from having sexual relations with a captive female slave whom he did not marry? We have already suggested that the phrase וְלָקַחְתָּ לְךָ לְאִשָּׁה belongs to the protasis rather than to the apodosis. That being the case, there is nothing

---

11   The verb גלח, "to shave," is found in connection with mourning rituals three times. Each time, however, it is the beard, not the head, which is shaved, so that קרח, "to make oneself bald," could not be used. Where the act of mourning involves shaving one's head, the verb used is quite consistently קרח. Moreover, there is no instance in the Hebrew Bible of a woman making herself bald as a mourning ritual.

12   Smith, *Deuteronomy*, 254.

13   See Deut 20:10ff.; Num 31:9; 1 Kgs 20:39; 2 Chron 28:8ff.; Is 14:2. For further discussion of enslaved prisoners in the ancient Near East, see Ignace J. Gelb, "Prisoners of War in Early Mesopotamia," *JNES* 32 (1973): 70-98.

in the law which prohibits the man from engaging in sexual relations with the woman without marrying her. Rather, the law simply sets forth a procedure for marrying the woman, should that be what the man chooses.

### b. *Deuteronomy 21:14*

The status of the captive woman is established in the last clause of v. 13; she is now the man's wife. Verse 14 rules that if the husband should cease to desire her, he must let her go.[14] As a wife, she cannot be sold.[15]

The *hithpael* stem of עמר is found only here and in Deut 24:7, where a man who steals another and sells him is subject to the death penalty. Its meaning is not certain. Alt argues plausibly, on the basis of a Ugaritic parallel, that the root was basically an economic term which meant something like "exercising power of disposal."[16] In any case, the law does constitute a limitation of the man's prerogatives over his wife, prohibiting a power of disposal which he might have expected to have.

The motive clause given in 21:14, תַּחַת אֲשֶׁר עִנִּיתָהּ, "because you have had your way with her," is problematic. The verb ענה, here translated "you have had your way with her," is used of sexual intercourse twelve times in the Hebrew Bible. In none of these instances (with the possible exception of our passage) does it refer to legally sanctioned sexuality. Most often it refers to an act of rape (2 Sam 13:12, 14, 22; Lam 5:11; Judg 19:24; 20:5); once to adulterous sex with a consenting woman (Deut 22:24); twice to violating an unbetrothed girl whose consent or lack of consent is not mentioned (Gen 34:2; Deut 22:29); once to sexual intercourse with a woman during her menstrual period (Ez 22:10); and once to incest (Ez 22:11). The word refers to sexual acts which are in some way illicit and are seen as debasing the woman. The relationship established by Deut 21:10-13, however, is legal not illicit. It may be that the drafters of the law viewed the marriage as an imposition on the woman since she was a captive, or they may have regarded marriage by cohabitation rather than by contract as not quite valid. In any case, the motive clause seems to

---

14    The *piel* stem of the verb שלח is used in Deuteronomy both as a technical term for divorce (22:19; 22:29; 24:1, 3-4) and for letting an indentured servant go (15:12). Here, the verb may carry both meanings. The phrase לְנַפְשָׁהּ, "as she wills," however, indicates that the stress is on letting her go free.

15    Cf. Ex 21:8, 11.

16    Albrecht Alt, "Zu Hit'ammēr," *VT* 2 (1952): 153-159. The *piel* participle of עמר is found in Ps 129:7 to mean "binding sheaves." Alt seeks a common root for these three instances and for a Ugaritic cognate found in lists of men subject to military conscription by the king. He adopts the suggestion made by Madeleine David, "Hit'āmēr (Deut 21:14; 24:7)" *VT* 1 (1951): 219-221, that the three biblical instances of the word could be taken as expressions of a root having to do with commercial transactions, and expands it to "power of disposal" in order to account for the Ugaritic text as well.

indicate that while the law provides a way for the man to marry a captive woman and later to divorce her if he no longer desires her, it sees the marriage or the divorce as in some way violating her.[17]

c. *Social and Familial Patterns Presupposed by the Law*

The law clearly assumes a male dominated situation. It addresses the male. It assumes that the male is the primary actor: he desires and takes, he no longer desires and sends out. While it defines the woman's legal status (wife) and provides her protection in that status (she may not be sold), it does so by limiting the man's actions.

The captive bride is clearly subordinate, but she is nonetheless viewed as a person with clearly defined rights (she may not be sold) rather than as chattel. She is a subject; she performs the ritual actions which effect her change in status from captive to member of the household. The man's humiliation of or imposition on the woman is recognized by the motive clause. Acknowledging that she can be imposed upon acknowledges her personhood; chattel cannot be debased.

### 3. *The Law of Primogeniture: Deuteronomy 21:15-17*

a. *Purpose*

Deut 21:15-17, the law of primogeniture, is not directly concerned with women. It is relevant to this study, however, because it also limits the authority of the male head of household in order to protect the rights of a dependent member of the family. In this case, it is the birthright of the chronologically first-born son which is protected.

The law presupposes that the first-born son customarily inherited the largest share of his father's estate.[18] The phrase מִשְׁפַּט הַבְּכֹרָה indicates

---

17    Frymer-Kensky, "Law and Philosophy," 100 n. 9, believes that in this case the man humiliates the woman by not going ahead with the marriage. ענה used of women elsewhere in Deuteronomy, however, has to do with sexual abasement. Moreover, the striking similarity between the motive clauses in Deut 21:14 and 22:29 makes it extremely unlikely that the same verb could refer to imposing sexual relations on the woman in the one case (22:29) and withholding sexual relations in the other.

18    The amount of the father's estate which a first-born son would inherit is a matter of debate. The Hebrew פִּי שְׁנַיִם, found here, in 2 Kgs 2:9 and in Zech 13:8, has several semitic cognates which establish its original meaning as "two-thirds" (see Paul Watson, "A Note on the 'Double Portion' of Deuteronomy 21:17 and 2 Kings 2:9," *Restoration Quarterly* 8 [1965]: 70-75). It came to mean "two parts" and hence, a "double portion." This is reflected in the LXX translation of Deut 21:17 and 2 Kgs 2:9, the Mishna, and the Talmud. Watson cites Zech 13:8 where the phrase must mean "two-thirds" as evidence that in this passage and the passage in 2 Kgs the phrase retains its original meaning. If that were so, it would have implications for this study, in that the law could represent an effort to consolidate patriarchal power along with the consolidation of property (cf. J. Henninger, "Premier-Nés en

the existence of an already established right or set of rights belonging to
the first-born. (A similar phrase found in Ex 21:9, מִשְׁפַּט הַבָּנוֹת, seems
similarly to indicate customary rights belonging to freeborn young
women.[19]) The law seeks to safeguard the chronologically eldest son by
prohibiting the father from arbitrarily assigning the rights of the first-born
to a younger son. Like the law of the captive bride, the law assumes the
authority of the male head of household and seeks to limit that
authority.[20]

The law is not primarily or directly aimed at safeguarding the rights of
an unloved wife, despite the claims of many scholars. Pierre Buis and
Jacques Leclercq see it as legislating equal treatment for wives in a
polygynous marriage.[21] Rofé believes that it is one of a series of laws

---

ethnologie," *DBS*, 481). Davies, however, correctly argues that in Old Testament
Hebrew פִּי like יַד is fractional only if it complements another fraction, and
otherwise has a multiplicative meaning (Eryl Davies, "The Meaning of *Pî Šenayim* in
Deuteronomy 21:17," *VT* 36 [1986]: 341-345). It is preferable, therefore, in the
absence of a complementary fraction, to translate the phrase as "two portions."

Extra-legal biblical material confirms that the privileged position of the first-born
was well established in Israel. Genealogical texts show that the family line is
continued through him (see Jacob Milgrom, "First-born," *IDBSup*, 337-338). The
term בְּכוֹר (first-born) cannot be transferred to a younger son (though the בְּכֹרָה
[birthright] may be). Reuben, though he has lost his birthright, continues to be called
the בְּכוֹר (1 Chron 5:1-2) and Shimri is not the בְּכוֹר, even though his father made
him chief (1 Chron 26:10).

The narrative materials give a rather mixed picture. There is a strong theme of
the elevation of the younger son; Abel is elevated over Cain, Jacob over Esau,
Joseph over Reuben, Ephraim over Manasseh, Moses over Aaron, David over his
brother, and Solomon over Adonijah. This theme runs throughout the OT
narratives. The stories of reversal, however, serve aetiological or theological
purposes, and assume that the privileged status of the first-born son was an
established custom.

The nature of the first-born's privilege apparently was not established with any
consistency. That it included inheritance rights can be seen in the Joseph-
Ephraim-Manasseh story. Through Jacob's adoption of Ephraim and Manasseh,
Joseph is given a double share of the inheritance. In Gen 48:22, Joseph is given a
*shechem* (hill) in addition to his share of his father's estate. 1 Chron 5:1-2 shows this
was at least interpreted as Joseph having been given the birthright. The stories
depicting the elevation of the younger son indicate that the father did previously
have the authority to transfer the birthright to a younger son.

19   For the translation "freeborn young women," see Shalom M. Paul, *Studies in the
     Book of the Covenant in the Light of Cuneiform and Biblical Law* (Leiden: E. J. Brill,
     1970), 55.

20   The wording of the law: לֹא יוּכַל לְבַכֵּר אֶת־בֶּן־הָאֲהוּבָה עַל־פְּנֵי בֶן־הַשְּׂנוּאָה הַבְּכֹר
     indicates that the acknowledgment of the father is necessary for the first-born son to
     receive his inheritance. The law recognizes the father's authority; it then seeks to
     direct how he shall use it.

21   Pierre Buis and Jacques Leclercq, *Le Deutéronome*, Sources Bibliques (Paris: J.
     Gabalda, et Cie, 1963), 149.

specifically concerned with women.[22] The law does repeatedly speak of a loved and an unloved wife. It does so, however, in a polemical way which suggests that the law was drafted against an actual practice.[23] The references to "loved" and "unloved" wives are more properly explained by the situation which the law is intended to counter. It is most likely that the prohibition applies to any attempt by the father to arbitrarily transfer the rights of the first-born to a younger son.

Certainly the amount of her son's inheritance would affect a mother's welfare. The question of a law's impact, however, differs from the question of its intent. This law quite explicitly intends to protect the status of the eldest son: "The birthright belongs to him."[24]

### b. Social and Familial Patterns Presupposed by the Law

The law, written in third-person, does not directly address anyone. It depicts the father as the primary actor (the father apportions his property) and seeks to regulate his behavior. The rights of the first-born son (like the rights of the captive bride) are protected indirectly, by limiting the prerogatives of the father.

It also assumes that the normal line of succession will be from father to son. This law does not, however, speak to the question of whether daughters could inherit in the absence of sons in pre-exilic times. The law envisions the existence of two sons; the issue of daughters possibly inheriting is outside of the purview of this passage.

The law, of course, also assumes the practice of polygyny. It perceives multiple wives as potential threats to the normal line of succession, and thus to social stability.

### 4. The Rebellious Son: Deuteronomy 21:18-21

### a. Purpose

Deut 21:14 and 21:15-17 seek to limit the prerogatives of the husband/father and to safeguard and extend protection to his dependents. Deut 21:18-21 prohibits a dependent son's rebellious behavior, and reasserts the inviolable authority of father and mother over their offspring. It does so by legislating the parents' right and possibly the parents' responsibility to bring their rebellious son to justice.

The law regards the parents' right to obedience as a matter of utmost

---

22  Rofé, "Family and Sex Laws," 131-159.

23  Milgrom, "First-born," 338, notes that the language is polemical. The repetition of the terms "loved" and "unloved," its emphasis that the son of the hated one is first-born, and the two motive clauses serve the purpose of emphasis.

24  This is not to rule out the possibility that the law was intended to serve other overarching purposes, such as keeping the family's estate as intact as possible, or supporting the stability of the family by minimizing squabbles over property.

concern to the larger community. The matter is handled publicly; it is brought before the elders at the gate. The rebellious son is to be stoned, a penalty in which all the men of the city participate. Finally, the use of the expurgation formula, "and you shall purge the evil from your midst," implies that toleration of the son's rebellious behavior would bring guilt on the entire community, and thus evoke God's wrath.

The offense against the parents is also an offense against God. The behavior condemned by the law is described as סוֹרֵר וּמוֹרֶה. Elsewhere in the Hebrew Bible סוֹרֵר always refers to Israel's (or its princes') rebellion against God. The gravity of the charge is not expressed by the word "stubborn." The Hebrew verb is used to describe apostasy, consistent refusal to obey Yahweh's commandments, flouting God's will. Found mainly in participial form, it refers not to a particular sinful deed, but to a continual rejection of divine will which amounts to a denial of divine authority and a rejection of relationship.

מוֹרֶה can refer to rebellion against another human being (cf. Josh 1:18); however, it almost always refers to rebellion against God. The rebellion is often against God's word, and can be contrasted with heeding God. Taken together, the two words describe ongoing rejection of authority. The son in this law, then, is charged with continually flouting his parents' will, with rebellion which constitutes a rejection of their authority and hence a rupture of the relationship. The terms express the opposite of כבד (Ex 20:12||Deut 5:16). They speak of rebellion against parents in terms which mirror the crime of rebelling against God. The authority of father and mother would seem in some way to reflect the authority of Yahweh.[25]

The passage is not aimed at limiting the father's power over his children. Some scholars have proposed that Deut 21:18-21 seeks to limit the authority of the father over his offspring, in that the law requires him to bring his son before the elders before he can inflict the death penalty

---

25  The parents appear to have the responsiblity as well as the right to bring their rebellious son to justice. This is indicated first by the expurgation formula, "you shall purge the evil from your midst," with its implied threat if justice is not carried out. It is also suggested by the second pair of charges brought against the son, זוֹלֵל וְסֹבֵא, that he is a glutton and a drunkard (v. 20). The first pair of charges, that he is recalcitrant and rebellious, directly concern the son's rejection of his parents' authority. This second set of charges is less directly related to disobeying his parents. Drunkenness and gluttony are socially disruptive behaviors. The inclusion of these charges may suggest that the parents were responsible for bringing to justice a son who violated the community's norms.

Elizabeth Bellefontaine, "Deuteronomy 21:18-21: Reviewing the Case of the Rebellious Son," *JSOT* 13 (1979): 13-31, esp. 20-24, has suggested that the two sets of charges reflect what were originally two different laws. The first would have concerned the violation of the authority of the parents; the second would have punished behavior intolerable to the community.

upon him. This interpretation is based, on the one hand, on the fact that the Deuteronomic law sets out the process by which the son can be tried[26] and, on the other, on the fact that there is evidence in the biblical stories that a father can have his dependents executed. There is, however, no evidence that a father's power over his dependents included the power of life and death in the later monarchical period.[27] Moreover, the rhetorical thrust of the law is not aimed at curbing the father's power. The law describes the process by which the son may be convicted, but it does not use polemical language in doing so. Rather, the gravity of the son's offense is emphasized by the language of the charge, the extreme penalty, and, in the law's final form, by the motive clauses. The law insists that the son must obey his parents. The authority of the father and mother over their offspring is thus resolutely upheld.

### b. *Social and Familial Patterns Presupposed by the Law*

The law sets out a process whereby the son may be tried. He is to be brought before the elders at the gate. His mother as well as his father are

---

26    The command to honor one's father and mother is obviously a central pillar of OT law. It is found in the center of the decalogue. The language of the fifth commandment (כבד) like the language of Deut 21:18 is language used of one's obligation to God. The gravity of dishonoring one's father and mother is seen in the death penalty prescribed for striking or cursing one's parents (Ex 21:15, 17; Lev 20:9). The injunction to honor parents, as well as the prohibition against dishonoring them, consistently refers to mother as well as father.

What is distinctive about Deut 21:18-21 is that it delineates the process whereby a son may be charged, convicted and punished. Because this process is not found elsewhere in biblical laws about the honor due one's parents, many commentators have assumed that ensuring due process for the accused son is the law's intent. They perceive it as designed to limit *patria potestas*. It is more likely, however, that the discussion of the process is part of the style of the Deuteronomic redactors, a style which may reflect the redactors' general concern for fair procedures. The same judicial process is set forth in Deut 25:7-10, which is clearly not intended to protect the rights of the reluctant levir, and in Deut 22:13-19, a law which is not primarily intended to make sure that a slanderous husband receives fair judicial process.

27    The father had extensive powers over dependent minors throughout ancient Israel's history. The father could sell his children into slavery, give them as surety, or punish them corporally (cf. Ex 21:7; Neh 5:2; Gen 42:37; Prov 19:18). Apparently a widowed mother could also give her children as surety (2 Kgs 4:1).

Judah's condemnation of Tamar (Gen 38:24) and Jacob's promise that whoever has Laban's household gods shall die (Gen 31:32) suggest that the father, in his capacity as judge over his household, could put his dependents to death. Both passages include legal terminology (לֹא יִחְיֶה, נכר); both include a sentence of death. These stories, however, are old. They are widely assumed to be older narratives incorporated by the Yahwist into his epic. There is no evidence that a father's power over his dependents included the power of life and death in the later monarchical period. Deut 21:18-21 is thus unlikely to be a Deuteronomic attempt to proscribe *patria potestas*.

plaintiffs. Strikingly, the verbs "take hold," "bring," and "speak" are in the plural. Both the mother and the father appear and speak in court. Furthermore, in continuity with pre-Deuteronomic legislation, the authority of the mother as well as the authority of the father is resolutely affirmed.

## 5. Conclusion

The three laws taken together thus express the Deuteronomic redactors' concern for the hierarchical authority of the family. They assert the authority of the father and the mother. Above all, they assume the authority of the male head of household. The laws also demonstrate a concern for the status and rights of dependent members of the hierarchically structured family.

# Chapter Two: Laws Concerning Adultery
## Deuteronomy 22:13-29

### 1. *Introduction*

Deut 22:13-29 is comprised of six laws which have been redacted into a single unit cohering around the theme of adultery.[1] The passage may be subdivided on the basis of style and content into three passages: 13-21 (two cases concerning charges that a bride was not virgin at marriage), 22-27 (adultery involving married or betrothed women), and 28-29 (violation of an unbetrothed girl).[2] We will first examine each of the three

---

1    The homogeneity of Deut 22:13-29 is widely recognized. the laws are unified at a redactional level by similarities of content, form, and wording. Each law has to do with a sexual offense. In contrast to the apodictic laws which precede and follow our passage, each of the laws comprising 22:13-29 is casuistic in form. Repeating terms also bind the laws into a single redactional unit. The *hiphil* stem of אָשֶּׁה, מצא, יצא, נַעֲרָה and בְּתוּלָה are used throughout the passage. The repetition of the death penalty and the expurgation formula, "you shall purge the evil from your midst," (v. 21, 22, 24) also contributes to the unity of the pericope. Moreover, the passage is defined by an inclusio. It begins with a case concerning premarital sexuality (22:13-19) and ends with a case concerning premarital sexuality (22:28-29). The penalties in both the first and last cases consist of a fine paid to the girl's father and the mandate that "she shall be his wife; he may not divorce her."

    Gordon J. Wenham and J.G. McConville, "Drafting Techniques in Some Deuteronomic Laws," *VT* 30 (1980): 248-252, have examined in some detail the techniques which the redactors used to unify this passage. They believe that the six laws were deliberately arranged to form two "panels," the first of which has to do with married women and the second of which has to do with unmarried girls. It is far from apparent that the נַעֲרָה בְתוּלָה מְאֹרָשָׂה, the betrothed virgin girl, of 22:23-24 and 25-27 should be categorized with the נַעֲרָה בְתוּלָה אֲשֶׁר לֹא־אֹרָשָׂה, the virgin girl who is not betrothed, as unmarried. Indeed, the fact that the death penalty is given for adultery with or by a betrothed girl indicates that, at least in relationship to third parties, she was considered married. Moreover, the terminology used in the laws does not support Wenham's and McConville's divisons. The "married woman" in Deut 22:13-21 is consistently referred to as נַעֲרָה, while the "unmarried woman" of 22:23-24 is called אָשֶּׁה. This study follows an alternative way of dividing the passage: (1) sexual intercourse prior to marriage (including prior to betrothal) discovered *ex post facto* (Deut 22:13-21); (2) sexual intercourse with a married or betrothed woman (Deut 22:22-27); and (3) sexual intercourse prior to betrothal, discovered at the time that it occurred.

    The following law, Deut 23:1 (Eng. 22:30) appears to have been attached to 22:13-29 because it also deals with a sexual offense. It differs from the laws in the preceding passage both in form and in content, and is not treated in this study. See p. 3 n. 11.

2    The unity of Deut 22:13-29 is the work of redactors. The passage is comprised of three distinct subunits, each of which appears to have its own tradition history. Deut

passages separately, and then discuss the purpose of the passage as a whole and the familial and legal status of women presupposed by it.

## 2. The Laws

### a. The Slandered Bride: Deuteronomy 22:13-21

This first passage is comprised of a case concerning the slander of a bride by her husband (v. 13-19) and its companion case, in which the bride is found guilty of her husband's charges (v. 20-21). The passage is obviously a unit; differences in style and content, however, have led to a near consensus that v. 20-21 have been added to the earlier case. The main case is repetitive and detailed; it is set before the elders. The sub-case has a compact style and lacks any references to the elders. The statement of the circumstances of the case in v. 13 assumes the girl's innocence, and thus fits the main case (13-19) but not the sub-case (20-21).[3]

The intent of the main case is shifted by the addition of the sub-case; we will consider the intent of the main case as it stands by itself, then in relationship to the sub-case.

---

22:13-19 and its companion law, v. 20-21, are distinguished from the rest of the passage by setting and style. Deut 22:13-19 takes place before the elders at the gate; it is characterized by repetition and direct speech. These stylistic considerations and the similarity of the law's style to Mesopotamian trial records have led Clemens Locher, "Deuteronomium 22:13-21 vom Prozessprotokoll zum Kasuitischen Gesetz," in *Das Deuteronomium*, ed. N. Lohfink, (Leuven: University Press, 1985), 298-303, to suggest that v. 13-19 were based on an actual trial; 20-21 (or 19b-21) would then have been added by the draftsman who turned the trial record into a caselaw. Locher's argument is persuasive. Although Locher does not say so, it seems possible that the draftsman who added v. 20-21 also redacted v. 22-29. Like v. 20-21, v. 22-29 define adultery, impose the death penalty, are written in a more compact style than v. 13-19a, and end with the expurgation formula.

The second section, v. 22-27, is comprised of three laws, each of which has parallels in the cuneiform codes. The three laws investigate the question of adultery by varying the woman's marital status and assent to the act in ways quite typical of ancient Near Eastern law. See Raymond Westbrook, *Studies in Biblical and Cuneiform Law* (Paris: J. Gabalda et Cie, 1988), 3-5.

The final law, v. 28-29, resembles v. 22-27 in style and form; it appears to have been reworked by the same redactor who drafted 22-27. It has biblical (Ex 22:15-16 [Eng. 22:16-17]) and cuneiform parallels (MAL A:55-56, *ANET*, 185), however, which indicate that the redactors have incorporated into their series on adultery a law which was earlier considered separate from the sexual offense laws. Moreover, v. 28-29 are distinguished from v. 22-27 by their content; the lawgiver intends to show that having sexual relations with an unmarried girl is not adultery, and thus does not result in the death penalty.

3    For a summary of scholarly discussion of the tensions between the two cases, see Locher, "Prozessprotokoll", 299.

The circumstances of the case are set forth in v. 13-14. Verse 13 is clear. A man takes a wife, consummates the marriage, then spurns her.[4] Verse 14 is more ambiguous. It describes the husband's accusations against his wife. The terminology used to describe his allegations, however, leaves unclear whether he has formally charged his wife before the court, or whether he has slandered her in the community. The wording of the law leaves open the question of whether the husband is plaintiff or defendant. The meaning of the phrase עֲלִילֹת דְּבָרִים is not clear. Following Dillmann, most modern commentators translate it either "wanton deeds," referring to the acts of which the husband has accused his bride, or "wanton words," in which case the phrase refers to the husband's false accusations.[5] Either interpretation fits the context well, but neither indicates whether the charges are to be understood as slander in the community or formal charges in the court. Likewise, the phrase וְהוֹצִיא עָלֶיהָ שֵׁם רָע, "bring against her an evil name," does not conclusively indicate that the husband has charged her before the elders.

The nature of the husband's accusations is related to the question of whether the husband or the parents brought the case before the elders. Roles in ancient Near Eastern court cases appear to have been much more flexible than roles in contemporary American courts of law. The one who brought the case before the elders could become the one accused.[6] Nonetheless, there must be a party who initiates the case. It does make some difference whether the husband or the parents bring the matter to court. Has the husband falsely and formally charged his bride before the elders, thus jeopardizing her life, or have the parents charged their son-in-law with spreading rumors about their daughter?

---

4    The term שׂנא belongs to the technical language for divorce (cf. Deut 24:3: "and the latter husband spurns her, and writes a bill of divorce for her, and sends her out"). The term came to be used alone (elliptically) to mean divorce at Elephantine (Reuven Yaron, *Introduction to The Law of the Aramaic Papyri* [Oxford: Clarendon Press, 1961], 55, 101). Its Akkadian equivalent, *zêru*, is found alone with the meaning "divorce" in documents from Old Babylonia, Alalakh, and Neo-Assyria (Raymond Westbrook, "Old Babylonian Marriage Law," vol. 2 [Ph.D. diss., Yale University, 1982]). In Biblical Hebrew, שׂנא used by itself *may* refer to the act of divorce in Judg 15:2. It is just possible (given the judgment in Deut 22:19 that "she shall be his wife") that in 22:13, שׂנא refers to the act of divorce, and that the situation is to be understood as a husband having divorced his wife, and being ordered by the elders to remarry her. Deuteronomy elsewhere, however, uses the *piel* stem of שׁלח to refer to divorce. It is better, therefore, to interpret שׂנא as referring to the emotion which motivates rejection rather than to an action.

5    Aug. Dillman, *Numeri, Deuteronomium und Josua*, 1886, cited by Driver, *Deuteronomy*, 254-255.

6    See Hans Boecker, *Law and the Administration of Justice in the Old Testament and the Ancient Near East*, trans. Jeremy Moiser (Minneapolis: Augsburg, 1980), 31-35. See also Deut 25:1; the judges could declare either party right or wrong.

The structure of the law seems to indicate that the parents of the girl are the plaintiffs in this case. Deut 22:13-19 is formally very similar to Deut 21:18-21 and 25:5-10. Each of these laws is set before the elders at the gate. In each law, a description of the case is followed by instruction to persons to come before the elders and make statements. The words that they are to say echo the previous description of the case. In Deut 21:18-21 and 25:5-10, the persons instructed to come and speak at the gate are unambiguously the plaintiffs; the words they are instructed to say are formal charges. In both of these cases, the penalty is levied against the person who was originally accused. In Deut 22:13-19, it is the girl's parents who are instructed to come before the elders and her husband who is penalized. We may assume, therefore, that the parents are the plaintiffs. That in turn indicates that the husband's "wanton words" were slander spoken in the community rather than false charges before the court.

The issue has significance for understanding Deuteronomy's view of women's legal status. Studies of Deut 21:13-21 often point out a possible inconsistency between the penalty in this case and the ruling found in Deut 19:16-19, the law against false witness.[7] Deut 19:16-19 mandates that anyone who brings false charges against another member of the community must suffer the penalty that the wrongly accused person would have suffered had the charge not been disproven. The husband in Deut 22:13-19 has made accusations against his wife which if proven true will result in her death (22:20-21). If these accusations comprise false testimony before the court, then the husband should be sentenced to death when his lies are discovered. According to v. 19, however, the husband is to be fined and possibly flogged. The discrepancy has been interpreted as evidence that Deut 19:16-19 applied only "to the testimony of one man against another" and that women were accorded no such safeguard.[8]

The inconsistency is more apparent than real. Deut 19:16-19 clearly concerns the situation where someone has brought false charges against someone else in court. We have argued that Deut 22:13-19 has to do with charges of slander brought by the girl's parents against her husband. The husband would be guilty of spreading malicious rumors but not of false testimony before the elders.

---

7    Locher, "Prozessprotokoll," 299, summarizes scholarly discussion of this issue.

8    Don C. Benjamin, *Deuteronomy and City Life* (Lanham: University Press of America, 1983), 229. More frequently, scholars cite the discrepancy between 22:13-21 and 19:16-19 as an indication that 22:13-21 is composite (Locher, "Prozessprotokoll," 299). Clemens Locher, *Die Ehre Einer Frau im Israel*, Orbis Biblicus et Orientalis, 70, (Goettingen: Vandenhoeck & Ruprecht, 1986), 373-380, also concludes that Deut 22:13-21 contradicts the principle of talion set forth in Deut 19:16-19.

It is even possible that 22:13-21 is intended to show that the law of false witness (Deut 19:16-19) does *not* apply in cases of slander. Phillips argues that Deut 22:13-19 specifically protects the slanderous husband by regarding his action as a financial offense against the girl's father and an injury to the honor of the girl's father, rather than as an attempt to have the girl put to death.[9] By this interpretation, the law would at the same time protect the bride and her father from slander and protect the slanderous husband from the most grave repercussions.

We have argued that Deut 22:13-19 concerns a husband who slanders his new bride in the community. The content of the husband's slander must still be clarified. What are the בְּתוּלִים which the husband has failed to find, and what does it mean that he cannot find them? Traditionally, בְּתוּלָה has been translated as "virgin"; בְּתוּלִים has been translated "tokens of virginity." The traditional translation of the Hebrew word בְּתוּלָה has been challenged by Wenham, who argues that the word must be translated "girl of marriageable age."[10] Wenham then interprets בְּתוּלִים as tokens that the girl was sexually mature; that is, as menstrual blood. By his reading of Deut 22:13-21, the husband, some time after he married the girl, charges that he has not found any signs that she has menstruated during the period of their marriage. That is to be understood as a charge that she was pregnant at the time he married her. Wenham thinks that the charge against the girl is that she became pregnant during the period of her betrothal. Her offense, then, was adultery.[11]

---

9    Phillips, *AICL*, 115 n. 28. A similar ambiguity is found in the CH. There also the laws concerning adultery are preceded by a law prohibiting slander against a woman (CH 127, *ANET* 171). The penalty for the false accuser is flogging and having half of his hair shaved off as a form of humiliation. If the accusation is assumed to be adultery, however (as the placement of the law would seem to indicate), then CH 127 is in some tension with CH 3, *ANET*, 166, which calls for a false witness to be executed. According to Driver and Miles, it is not clear, however, that the slanderer has testified in court rather than gossiped in the neighborhood (Godfrey R. Driver and John C. Miles, eds., *The Babylonian Laws*, vol. 1 [Oxford: Clarendon Press, 1952], 276-277). They view the wording of CH 127, "if a man pointed a finger," as a gesture of the street rather than of the court. CH 127 appears to have the same dual function of protecting the woman from slander while limiting the liability of the slanderer.

10   Gordon J. Wenham, "*Bĕtûlāh* 'A Girl of Marriageable Age,'" *VT* 22 (1972): 326-348. Wenham based his work in part on the arguments of Benno Landsberger, "Jungfräulichkeit: Ein Beitrag zum Thema 'Beilager und Eheschliessung,'" in *Symbolae Juridicae et Historicae Martino David Dedicatae* (Leiden: E. J. Brill, 1968), 41-105, and the position of Jacob J. Finkelstein, "Sex Offenses in Sumerian Laws," *JAOS* 86 (1966): 356-357, that the Akkadian term *batultu* indicates the girl's age rather than her virginity.

11   If Wenham's interpretation were correct, the case in Deut 22:20-21 would be a specific instance of adultery committed by a betrothed girl (Deut 22:23-24). That is, Deut 22:20-21 would have to do with a case of adultery by a betrothed girl which was not discovered until after her marriage, and which resulted in pregnancy. By that

The traditional view is the more convincing interpretation. Because the question has significance for understanding the view of women found within the Deuteronomic code, and because Wenham's position has garnered support, we will refute Wenham in some detail.[12]

Wenham argues that בְּתוּלָה denotes a girl of a certain age rather than a virgin. His argument seems valid for the term as it is generally used. There are poetic and narrative passages where the translation "virgin" for בְּתוּלָה is either impossible or unlikely. Joel 1:8 reads: "Lament like a בְּתוּלָה girded in sackcloth for the בַּעַל of her youth." בַּעַל is not elsewhere used in the Hebrew Bible to refer to a prospective bridegroom. When used of the male/ female relationship, it regularly means "husband." Here, then, the woman has been married; the translation "virgin" is excluded. Moreover, in Gen 24:16 and Judg 21:12 (as Wenham points out) a girl described as a בְּתוּלָה is further described as one whom "no man has known," or "who had not known men by lying with them." Wenham rightly asserts that the relative clauses would be redundant if בְּתוּלָה already denoted that the girl was a virgin. That the basic meaning of בְּתוּלָה is "girl of marriageable age" has been widely accepted.[13]

Words often acquire technical meanings when they are used in a legal context. Wenham's argument no longer holds when one considers the use of the term בְּתוּלָה within the laws. Several of the laws require understanding בְּתוּלָה with the more specialized meaning, "virgin." Lev

---

interpretation, Deut 22:20-21 would not add anything new to the definition of adultery found in Deut 22:22-27. We interpret the law as applying to any bride who is unchaste. According to our view, the law does contribute to the Deuteronomic definition of adultery. That is, for a girl to enter a first marriage without her virginity intact is a capital offense regardless of whether the sexual intercourse took place before or after her betrothal. The husband's claim over his wife's sexuality is retroactive; it extends to the period before their betrothal.

The interpretation of the passage may also influence one's understanding of the purpose of the adultery laws in general. By Wenham's reading of the passage, the offense committed by the girl which warrants the death penalty is entering into marriage pregnant by a man other than her husband. If pregnancy were the heart of her offense, the connection between the adultery laws and concern for paternity would be that much clearer. The traditional reading of the law (that the heart of the girl's offense is her lack of virginity) does not exclude paternity from the concern of the adultery laws. It does, however, give more weight to the concern of the law for the father or husband's authority over the girl.

12   For example, Andrew D. H. Mayes, *Deuteronomy*, New Century Bible (Grand Rapids: Eerdmans, 1981), 310, follows Wenham in interpreting the girl's offense as being pregnant at the time of her marriage.

13   Matitiahu Tsevat, "*Bĕtûlāh*," *TDOT* vol. 2, 338-343; Harry M. Orlinsky, "Virgin," *IDBSup*, 939-940; Mayes, *Deuteronomy*, 312; and Peggy Day, "From the Child Is Born the Woman: The Story of Jephthah's Daughter," in *Gender and Difference in Ancient Israel*, 58-74, hold that the basic meaning of בְּתוּלָה is "girl of marriageable age." They argue that the term has the more specialized meaning, "virgin," in some contexts.

21:13-14 (which mandates what kinds of women the high priest may marry) places the בְּתוּלָה in opposition to the widow, divorcee, defiled woman or harlot. Ez 44:22 rules that a priest shall marry a בְּתוּלָה or a widow of a priest, but not a layman's widow or a divorcee. The opposition of the terms clearly suggests that one read בְּתוּלָה as "virgin." Wenham's attempt to argue that "girl of marriageable age" is a less redundant translation than "virgin" is strained. Moreover, it would be difficult to understand why the high priest must marry a girl of marriageable age while the regular priests need not do so.[14] It is easy to understand how the priestly writers would require the high priest, of whom the most holiness was demanded, to marry a virgin.

These passages have led several scholars to suggest that בְּתוּלָה came to have a specialized meaning "virgin" in at least some of the biblical laws.[15] Such a development has analogies in the Greek *parthenos* and Latin *virgo* which developed from the more general meaning "maiden" to the specialized meaning "virgin."[16]

A specialized meaning of בְּתוּלִים as "tokens of virginity" must be accepted for Deut 22:13-21. Wenham's explanation of the בְּתוּלִים as menstrual blood and the husband's charge, that he had failed to find signs that she was menstruating, is implausible for several reasons.

First, Wenham's interpretation of the husband's accusation is implausible on the face of it. By his interpretation, the husband says in effect, "I had sexual intercourse with my wife and now, some weeks later, she shows signs of being pregnant." It is difficult to understand why it would be assumed that the husband was not the father, or why the husband would express an accusation that his bride was pregnant at the time of their marriage in such an indirect and unlikely fashion.

Second, the plain reading of v. 14 is to assume that the husband's "drawing near" to his bride refers to sexual intercourse. The husband could reasonably expect to find hymenal blood after intercourse with his new bride. Wenham's interpretation that the husband drew near to his wife to see if she were menstruating is strained.

Finally, Wenham's reading of Deut 22:20-21 makes it simply a specific instance of adultery committed by a betrothed girl. That offense is discussed in Deut 22:23-24. Such repetition is not elsewhere found in

---

14    Lev 21:7 prohibits priests from marrying harlots, defiled women, or women divorced from their husbands; it does not prohibit their marrying widows, nor does it require them to marry a בְּתוּלָה.

15    Locher, *Die Ehre Einer Frau*, 121-238, has argued this at great length, although he unfortunately limits his discussion to Deut 22:13-21 and comparative cuneiform material without considering the term in the context of other biblical laws. Tsevat, "*Bĕtûlāh*," and Orlinsky, "Virgin," each argue that בְּתוּלָה and בְּתוּלִים must be translated "virgin" and "virginity" at least in Lev 21:13-14; Ez 44:22; and Deut 22:13-21.

16    Tsevat, "*Bĕtûlāh*," 340.

Deuteronomy 19-25. The traditional reading, that the husband accuses his wife of not being virgin at the time of their wedding, is much more likely.

The apodosis of the law (apart from the question of the nature of the בְּתוּלִים) is fairly straightforward. It is noteworthy that the mother as well as the father presents the evidence to the elders, although, in contrast to Deut 21:20, only the father speaks. A dual penalty is imposed on the slanderous husband: he must pay damages of one hundred shekels, which are given to the father of the girl, and he may never divorce the girl.[17]

The fine of one hundred shekels suggests that financial concerns may well underlie the law. The husband may have slandered his bride in order to fraudulently reclaim the money which he had paid for her.[18] Marriages were contracted through the payment of a bridewealth by the groom to the father of bride (cf. Gen 34:12; Ex 22:15; 1 Sam 18:25).[19] The cuneiform codes allow a groom to reclaim double the amount which he had paid if his father-in-law failed to follow through on the contract by delivering his daughter.[20] Presumably a groom could also claim breach of contract and thus recover double the bridewealth if he found that the girl was not a virgin. The fifty shekels paid by the violator of an unmarried virgin (Deut 22:28-29) is likely to be a fixed sum for the bridewealth.[21] The hundred shekels fine which the slanderous husband has to pay and which is given to the father of the bride would then be double the bridewealth. The husband is thus fined the amount that the father of the

---

17   יִסְּרוּ has traditionally been understood to mean "flog"; some support for that reading is found in MAL 18, *ANET*, 181, where the penalty for slander seems to include flogging. Elsewhere in the Hebrew Bible, however, the verb יסר most often means "admonish" or "punish." יסר probably means "punish" in this text also. The following verse defines the punishment as a fine. (So Mayes, *Deuteronomy*, 310.)

18   This is the position of Mayes, *Deuteronomy*, 309.

19   The nature of the bridewealth and its implications for the nature of marriage in the ancient Near East has been a subject of intense scholarly debate. It has been interpreted as the price of the purchase of a bride, a compensation gift for the loss of a daughter (Millar Burrows, *The Basis of Israelite Marriage*, [New Haven: American Oriental Society, 1938]); as necessary proof of marriage (A. van Praag, *Droit Matrimonial Assyro-Babylonien*, [Amsterdam: Noord-Hollandsche Uitgervers Maatschappij, 1945], 147-148); and interpreted in relationship to the model of payment for adoption (Westbrook, OMBL, vol. 2, 152-157). An examination of the nature of the bridewealth in ancient Israel, and thus of the nature of Israelite marriage, per se, is beyond the scope of this study. One may briefly note that it is clear that the institution of marriage, and the nature of the *terhatum* (Akkadian bridewealth) or *mohar* (Hebrew bridewealth) is different at different time periods and different geographical regions. It is also clear that in at least some regions and periods, including some periods in ancient Israel, the bridewealth was a real and not merely a symbolic payment. This is indicated by the negotiations between Shechem and Jacob, Gen 34.

20   CE 25, *ANET*, 162; CH 160, *ANET*, 173; HL 29, *ANET*, 190.

21   See below, p. 39.

girl would have to pay if the charges were upheld and the contract proved to have been broken.

The fact that the law may have to do with a financial conflict does not deny that it is primarily about slander. In the course of his attempted fraud, the husband has tarnished the honor of his father-in-law's family. The nature of the offense is emphasized by the repetition of the phrases שֵׁם רָע (v. 14, 19) and עֲלִילֹת דְּבָרִים (14, 17), the repetition of the charge "I did not find ... the tokens of virginity," v. 14 and 17, and the explanatory clause of v. 19, "he has brought an evil name upon a virgin of Israel."

The dual nature of the penalty imposed on the husband (damages paid to his father-in-law and prohibition against ever divorcing his wife) raises another question. Who does the law consider to have been wronged by the husband's accusations? The father receives the damages even though the motive clause cites the evil name brought upon the girl as the basis for that penalty. Indeed, the father is compensated at the girl's expense; the damages paid to her father are taken from the household to which she is now permanently attached. The law apparently views the father and his household as an injured party.[22]

The law also prohibits the husband from ever divorcing his spurned wife, and thus provides her with some social/economic security. Since Israelite men apparently could divorce their wives at will, the prohibition is to be seen as a penalty imposed on the husband which protects the wife. The law thus also treats the girl as an injured party. One notes, however, that this penalty benefits the girl's father as well as the girl, in that it assigns responsibility for providing for her to the husband rather than to the father. The penalties acknowledge that the husband has offended both the father and the daughter.

Deut 22:13-19, then, provides for the father (and mother) of a bride who is slandered by her husband to bring charges against the slanderer, and to receive compensation from him for the dishonor brought upon her father and his family. It further penalizes the slanderer by forcing him to provide for the woman for the rest of their lives.

The sub-case (v. 20-21) is concerned with the situation where the husband's accusations are true; the girl was not a virgin when she was married. These verses were secondarily added to the primary case. In

---

22    If the husband's attempt to recover his bridewealth is an underlying concern of the law, then the nature of the offense against the father is very clear. The husband has attempted to commit fraud against his father-in-law. It is easy to understand, however, that even the explicit concern of the law, slander, is an offense against the father. The father's honor requires that he be able to control his daughter's sexuality. The relationship of male honor and female sexuality is clear in the Shechem narrative (Gen 34); it is discussed at some length by Julian Pitt-Rivers, *The Fate of Shechem; or, the Politics of Sex: Essays in the Anthropology of the Mediterranean*, Cambridge Studies in Social Anthropology, no. 19 (Cambridge: Cambridge University Press, 1977), esp. 161-168.

them the focus of the laws shifts from slander to sexual offense. The defendant shifts from the husband to the girl. (It is not clear who prosecutes the case in v. 20-21.) Assuming that we have interpreted בְּתוּלִים correctly, the purpose of this sub-case is to include entering into a first marriage as a non-virgin among the sexual offenses punishable by death. That is, it extends the husband's exclusive rights over his wife's sexuality to her life before their betrothal. "A woman's sexuality was understood to belong to her husband alone, for whom it must be reserved in anticipation of marriage as well as in the marriage bond."[23]

The gravity of the girl's offense is made clear by the penalty: death. That it is an offense against the community as well as against her husband and father is seen in the fact that she is to be executed by all of the men of her city.

The seriousness and the social dimension of the offense are further underlined by the explanatory clause (v. 21). For a girl to enter into a first marriage without her virginity intact is termed a נְבָלָה בְּיִשְׂרָאֵל. That is (as Phillips has shown) it is deemed a crass violation which seriously threatens the social order.[24]

The offense is described by the phrase לִזְנוֹת בֵּית אָבִיהָ,[25] that is, to engage in illicit sexual relations while under the authority of her father.[26] The second phrase is in apposition to the first: by flouting the authority of her father by engaging in sexual relations while part of his household, the girl has committed a crass offense which threatens the social order of Israel. The expurgation formula (v. 21b) reinforces the gravity of the offense, its social implications, and the responsibility of the (male) community of Israel to eradicate the evil.[27]

---

23  Phyllis Bird, "To Play the Harlot: an Inquiry into an Old Testament Metaphor," in *Gender and Difference in Ancient Israel*, 77.

24  Anthony Phillips, "*Nebalah*--A Term for Serious Disorderly and Unruly Conduct," *VT* 25, (1975): 237-242. Other sexual offenses which are referred to as וְנְבָלָה include the violation of Dinah (Gen 34:7), the rape of the concubine and threatened rape of her master (Judg 19:23; 20:6), and the rape of Tamar by Amnon (2 Sam 13:12). Each of these offenses provoked a violent breakdown of social order. Only in this law is a woman's offense ever described as וְנְבָלָה.

25  The text is questionable at the word לִזְנוֹת. SamP has להזנות. LXX has *ekporneusai* which is used by the LXX to translate the infinitive of זנה in both the *hiphil* (Lev 19:29) and *qal* (Lev 20:6) stems. The *qal* infinitive is found in the targums. The weight of the evidence of the versions and the possibility of explaining SamP as a response to the difficulty of the absence of a preposition before "her father's house" favors the MT. (For the use of an accusative to answer the question "where?" without a preposition, see GKC, par. 118g.)

26  Bird, "To Play the Harlot," 77. The MT literally reads: "To fornicate in the household of her father," which is to be understood as "while a member of her father's household," that is, while under his authority.

27  Presumably the "men of her city" who are to stone her are the ones charged with purging the evil from the midst of the community.

The law views the girl's lack of virginity as an offense against Israel's order and her father's authority. The father has rights to dispose of her sexuality. By being placed with the laws concerning adultery, the girl's offense is also clearly though implicitly seen as an offense against her husband's exclusive rights to possession of her sexuality. Deut 22:28-29 and Ex 22:15-16 show that sexual intercourse between a man and an unbetrothed girl was not regarded as a capital offense. Apparently previous sexual activity becomes a capital offense if the girl then enters into a marriage with another man, who has the right to expect her to be a virgin.[28]

### b. *Adultery: Deuteronomy 22:22-27*

Deut 22:22-27 is comprised of three laws dealing with adultery with a married or betrothed woman (v. 22, 23-24, and 25-27). These laws look at the question of the treatment of adultery in light of two variables: (1) the girl's or woman's marital status and (2) her consent or lack of consent to the sexual act. Based on these two variables, the laws then determine the penalty.

Each of the three cases begins by carefully defining the woman's marital status. In v. 22, the woman is described as בְּעֻלַת בַּעַל. The phrase need not be translated as implying she is "owned by an owner." It does indicate that she is under the authority of a master/husband. The phrase is found only here and in Gen 20:3, where Abimelech is warned that Sarah is another man's wife. In both contexts, the wording emphasizes the husband's claims over his wife. It clearly specifies her marital status.

---

28   Rofé, "Family and Sex Laws," 131-158, holds that Deut 22:20-21 is in tension with the view of premarital sexual relations found in other biblical and ancient Near Eastern texts. He notes that other laws do not regard sexual relations with an unbetrothed girl as a serious crime. Moreover, he notes that Deut 22:20-21 does not distinguish between a girl who has lost her virginity because of rape and one who has consented to sexual relations. This, he argues, puts the law in tension with Deut 22:23-27 (and with the cuneiform laws concerning sexual offense).

Rofé interprets this tension between Deut 22:20-21 and other biblical/ancient Near Eastern laws as an indication that Deut 22:20-21 was not drafted by a law-giver nor intended to be put into practice. Rather, it was written by a moralist who wanted to preach sexual morality. To support his case, Rofé points to the similarity between Deut 22:20-21 and Deut 21:18-21 (which he also views as late preaching of morals rather than genuine law).

Rofé's observations of the similarity between the two laws are accurate. He is also correct when he notes that they both stress the authority of the father over his minor dependents. The tension between Deut. 22:20-21 and other legislation concerning premarital sexual offenses is not as great as Rofé believes that it is, however. Rofé overlooks the fact that the girl has not only been involved in premarital sexual activity; she has entered into a new marriage without acknowledging her loss of virginity. The facts of the case in 22:20-21 differ from those of 22:28-29.

Verse 23 uses three terms to specify the status of the girl in the next two laws; she is a נַעֲרָ בְתוּלָה מְאֹרָשָׂה. The meaning of the first two terms is debated.[29] One can be confident, however, that the presence of the terms indicates the concern of the draftsman to define the girl's status carefully. The term מְאֹרָשָׂה specifies that the girl is betrothed; that is, a man has paid the bridewealth for her, and thus has a claim to her.[30]

The second variable found in v. 23-24 and 25-27 is the consent or lack of consent of the woman. If a man has sexual intercourse with a girl in a city, she is presumed to have consented to the act. If he takes her in the countryside, she is presumed to have resisted. The site where the sexual offense takes place is also used to indicate the woman's consent or lack of consent in the Hittite laws.[31] That the variable of consent/non-consent is found only in the cases concerning a betrothed woman does not mean that the variable would be immaterial in the case of a married woman. Rather, the hearer would be expected to reason from the case of the betrothed girl to the case of the married woman.[32]

Finally, each case mandates the death penalty, and takes great care to specify who is liable. Verse 22 says that "indeed (גַּם), both of them ... the man ... and the woman" shall die. In the second case (involving a consenting, betrothed woman) the explanatory clauses of v. 24, together with the phrase שְׁנֵיהֶם, carefully indicate that both the man and the woman are to be stoned. The third case (involving a non-consenting

---

29   The thesis of Hans Peter Stähli's book, *Knabe-Jüngling-Knecht: Untersuchungen zum Begriff im Alten Testament*, (Frankfurt: Peter Lang, 1978), is that נער in both its masculine and feminine forms refers to a social status rather than to an age category. The debate concerning בְּתוּלָה has been discussed above.

30   The term is rare in the Hebrew Bible. Apart from Deuteronomic legislation, it is found in a literal sense only in 2 Sam 3:14, where David bases his demand that his wife Michal be returned to him on the fact that he paid the bridewealth for her. This narrative does give two pieces of information, however. First, ארשׂ involves payment. (BDB connect the verb with an Arabic noun for "a fine," and suggest it literally has to do with "paying the price of," 77.) Second, David bases his claim to Michal on the fact he had paid the bridewealth for her rather than the fact he had married her. This is consistent with the Deuteronomic laws, and with the picture of betrothal or, better, "inchoate marriage," which emerges from the cuneiform codes.

31   Par. 197, *ANET*, 196. Location is also important in MAL A:12-16, *ANET*, 181. There, however, it is mainly used as one indication of the man's guilt or blamelessness. If the woman is in a brothel or in the streets, and thus may be assumed to be presenting herself as a prostitute, the law provides for the possibility that the man may not have been aware of her marital status, and so would not be liable to charges of adultery.

32   So: Westbrook, *SBCL*, 6. Finkelstein, "Sex Offenses," 366-368, identifies a correlation between married women and consent and unmarried women and non-consent in the cuneiform codes. He suggests that the correlation reflects the youth of the unmarried girls who would therefore be unlikely to solicit sexual experience.

betrothed woman) uses five separate clauses to stress that the man alone is liable and the girl is to be held blameless.[33]

The laws, then, revolve around two variables: the marital status of the woman, and woman's consent or lack of consent. The first variable, the woman's marital status, defines the gravity of the offense. In Israel, as in the rest of the ancient Near East, adultery is defined as sexual relations between a married or betrothed woman and a man other than her husband. The second variable, the woman's consent or lack of consent, determines whether the woman, as well as the man, is held culpable.[34]

One must ask whether the liability of women to the law of adultery was a Deuteronomic innovation. Was one purpose of Deut 22:22-24 to make women who committed adultery liable to the community rather than to their husbands? Daube and Phillips argue that prior to the Deuteronomic law, a man who committed adultery would be executed by the community while his female counterpart was at the mercy of her husband. Phillips (but not Daube) believes that the husband had no right to have his wife put to death; at most he could divorce her.[35] They believe that Deuteronomy for the first time made women subject to laws against adultery. We will argue that Phillips' and Daube's positions cannot be sustained.

Phillips' and Daube's arguments are based in part on the rhetoric of the laws. They believe that the wording of Deut 22:22 emphasizes the liability of women to the law. Daube in particular argues that the apodosis of the law, וּמֵתוּ גַּם־שְׁנֵיהֶם הָאִישׁ הַשֹּׁכֵב עִם־הָאִשָּׁה וְהָאִשָּׁה, greatly stresses the fact that women as well as men are to be judged culpable.[36] Their argument is implausible. The phrasing does not necessarily indicate that including the woman in the penalty was innovative. Deut 22:22-27, like MAL 12-16,[37] delineates very precisely which of the parties is guilty under varying circumstances. The emphasis that Deut 22:22 places on the guilt of both parties is in keeping with the purpose of the law. Moreover, Daube places too much importance on the phrase גַּם־שְׁנֵיהֶם, which he

---

33  (1) The man *alone* shall die; (2) you shall do nothing to the girl; (3) there is no guilt deserving death in her; (4) this case is comparable to murder (underscoring the innocence of the victim); and (5) there was no one to help her if she cried out. The reference to the case of murder alludes to Deut 19:11 and is clearly secondary.

34  Finkelstein, "Sex Offenses," 366, has charted cuneiform and biblical sexual offense laws according to these two "axes of legal import." A third axis around which the cuneiform adultery laws revolve is the male adulterer's knowledge or ignorance of the woman's marital status (cf. YBC 2177, pars. 7-8, *ANET*, 526 and MAL A:14, *ANET*, 181).

35  Daube, "Biblical Landmarks," 177-180; Phillips, *AICL*, 110-112. Phillips believes that Judah's condemnation of Tamar is a late gloss. There is, however, no textual evidence for this position.

36  Daube, "Biblical Landmarks," 179.

37  *ANET*, 181.

believes puts great stress on the fact the woman is also to be executed. Against Daube's view, גַם שְׁנֵיהֶם is also found in Deut 23:19 (Eng. 23:18); Prov 17:15; and Prov 20:10, none of which places any special emphasis on one of the two elements in particular.

Phillips and Daube also base their arguments on some early narratives which depict the man, but not the woman, as culpable for adultery (Gen 12:11-20, Sarah and Pharaoh; Gen 20:2-18, Sarah and Abimelech; Gen 26:7-11, Rebekah and Abimelech.) In these three stories (or, rather, these variants of the same story) the patriarch asks his wife to pose as his sister and thus risks her being sexually used by the king or some other man. The king is horrified by the guilt which he and his people might have incurred; there is no indication that Sarah or Rebekah is considered liable.[38]

Daube's and Phillips' use of these narratives as evidence of Judean legal practice just prior to the Deuteronomic period is problematic. They are narratives about kings and patriarchs, not about ordinary Israelites.[39] The narratives are stories, shaped by both literary and theological purposes, not historical accounts or laws. Finally, they are set in the ancestral period and presumably reflect what later authors thought were the customs of that period; they certainly are not evidence of social and legal practices during or just prior to the Deuteronomic period.[40] It is unlikely that the inclusion of women in the penalty of Deut 22:22 is innovative.[41]

---

38    Daube, "Biblical Landmarks," 178. Daube cites the case of David and Bathsheba as evidence that the man but not the woman was considered criminally liable for adultery. He believes that both were guilty of the act, but that only David was punished. In fact, there is no evidence that Bathsheba could have refused David, and she was punished just as he was by the loss of their son.

      Phillips, *AICL*, 110-111, also cites Hos 2:4 and Jer 3:8 as evidence that prior to Deuteronomy, women caught in adultery were divorced rather than executed. Phillips' predeuteronomic dating of Jer 3:8 is unlikely. Jer 3:6ff. appears to be a late passage which depends on Jer 3:1-5; Jer 3:1-5 in turn depends upon Deut 24:1-4.

39    It is not clear, for example, that the woman could have refused a king. One therefore cannot speak of her liability or nonliability to the law.

40    For further discussion of the Daube and Phillips positions, see Arnold Anderson, "Law in Old Israel: Laws Concerning Adultery," in *Law and Religion: Essays on the Place of the Law in Israel and Early Christianity*, ed. Barnabas Lindars, (Cambridge: James Clarke & Co. 1988), 13-19, esp. 15-16.

41    Daube's and Phillips' arguments are situated within a larger debate concerning the history of Israelite legal practice concerning adultery. Moshe Greenberg, "Some Postulates of Biblical Criminal Law," *Yehezkel Kaufmann Jubilee Volume* (Jerusalem: Magnes Press, 1960), 5-28; Paul, *Studies in the Book of the Covenant*, 98; and Anthony Phillips, "Another Look at Adultery," *JSOT* 20 (1981): 3-25, maintain that Israel viewed adultery primarily as an offense against God, rather than as an offense against the husband. The offense therefore could not be pardoned. This is in contrast to the surrounding ancient Near Eastern cultures, where adultery was supposed to be viewed as an offense against the husband, who could pardon his wife and her paramour.

Rather, the Deuteronomic insistence that both the man and the woman who are guilty of adultery should be executed reflects the Deuteronomic view of the gravity of the offense. The three laws belong to an overall series of laws (22:13-29) which serves to identify what is or is not adultery. Within that context, the three laws in 22:22-27 focus specifically on who is or is not guilty, on the one hand, and emphasize the gravity of the event, on the other.

It is not clear from these laws who is expected to prosecute the adulterers. The identity of the executioners is more clear. Assuming that the redacters had in mind the same executioners for the different adultery laws, the penalty was intended to be carried out by "all of the men" of their respective cities. This in turn may provide a clue for the identity of the intended audience of the laws. The plural "you" in 22:24, "You shall bring the two of them out to the gate of that city and stone them," would be the group responsible for carrying out the execution, that is, the men of the city.

### c. *Violation of an Unbetrothed Girl: Deuteronomy 22:28-29*

Formally and stylistically, Deut 22:28-29 is closely knit to v. 22-27. Like the two previous cases, it begins with the phrase "if a man overtakes

---

Robert Gordis, "On Adultery in Biblical and Babylonian Law--A Note," *Judaism* 33, 2 (1984): 210-211; Bernard S. Jackson, "Reflections on Biblical Criminal Law," in *Essays in Jewish and Comparative Legal History*, (Leiden: E. J. Brill, 1975), 60-61; Samuel E. Loewenstamm, "The Laws of Adultery and Murder in Biblical and Mesopotamian Law," and "The Laws of Adultery and Murder in the Bible," in *Comparative Studies in Biblical and Ancient Oriental Literature*, AOAT 204 (Neukirchen-Vluyn: Neukirchener Verlag, 1980), 146-153, 171-172; Henry McKeating, "Sanctions Against Adultery in Ancient Israelite Society, with Some Reflections on Methodology in the Study of Old Testament Ethics," *JSOT* 11 (1979): 57-72; and Westbrook, *SBCL*, 97 n. 36, argue that the biblical laws mandating the death penalty for adultery (Deut 22:22-27; Lev 20:10) set forth the ideal or ultimate penalty. Israelite legal practice would have been similar to the practice of the surrounding cultures. That is, it was probably the wronged husband who prosecuted adultery; he could have pardoned the offense or imposed the lesser penalty of divorce on his wife.

The latter argument is the more persuasive. There are no instances of either a man or a woman being put to death for adultery in the Hebrew Bible. Moreover, there is evidence of lesser penalties imposed for adultery. Several prophetic writings (Hos 2:4-5 [Eng. 2:2-3]; Jer 3:8; Is 50:1) envision divorce as the penalty for an adulterous wife. Prov 6:32-35 seems to assume that the cuckolded husband determined the adulterer and adulteress's fate, and that he could choose to accept ransom in lieu of demanding the execution of the culprits.

The discrepancy between these passages and the uncompromising insistence on the death penalty in the biblical laws concerning adultery is best explained in terms of the difference between practice and ideal. The laws stress the utter seriousness of the offense.

a girl" (v. 23b, 25).[42] Like the previous laws, it includes a precise identification of the girl's marital status. In contrast to the נַעַר בְתוּלָה מְאֹרָשָׂה of v. 23-27, v. 28-29 treat the case of a נַעַר בְתוּלָה אֲשֶׁר לֹא־אֹרָשָׂה, a virgin girl who has not been betrothed.[43] The girl's unbetrothed status takes the case out of the sphere of capital offenses. Sexual intercourse with an unbetrothed girl is not adultery. Its penalty is not execution. Rather, the man must pay the girl's father fifty shekels, marry her, and is prohibited from ever divorcing her.

The violation of an unbetrothed virgin is also treated by a law in the Book of the Covenant, Ex 22:15-16. In the Exodus law also the violator is required to pay money to the father and marry the girl. Scholarly debate concerning Deut 22:28-29 has focused on the question of its relationship to Ex 22:15-16, that is, whether the two passages have to do with two different cases or are variants of the same case. In contrast to traditional interpreters, we will argue that the two passages are variants of the same case. In contrast to Weinfeld and several other contemporary scholars, we will argue that the differences between the two variants cannot be ascribed to the Deuteronomic authors' "humanitarian view of women."[44]

---

42   Anthony Ceresko, "The Function of *Antanaclasis* (mṣ' 'to find'//mṣ' 'to reach, overtake, grasp') in Hebrew Poetry, Especially in the Book of Qoheleth," *Catholic Biblical Quarterly* 44 (1982): 551-569, argues convincingly that the verb מצא actually represents two roots, one of which means "overtake," the other "find." Whether or not Ceresko is correct in positing two original roots, he is correct that מצא has been deliberately used in Deut 22:13-29 with a variety of shades of meaning from "discovered" to "overtaken." This use of the verb is one of the ways that the redactor shows both the connectedness and the variation of the different cases.

43   David Weiss, "A Note on אשר לא ארשה," *JBL* 81 (1962): 67-69, argues that the phrase לֹא־אֹרָשָׂה should be translated "has never been engaged" because the verb is a perfect passive. The emphasis would then not be on the contrast between the betrothed status of the girl in v. 23-27 and the unbetrothed status of the girl in v. 28-29 but on the fact that the girl in v. 28-29 had never been betrothed; her father had never received the bridewealth for her. Weiss reads too much into the contrast between the use of the participle in v. 23 and the perfect in v. 28. The similarity of the language and form of v. 23-27 and 28-29 indicates that the drafter of the laws was creating a deliberate contrast between the status of the girl in v. 23-27 and the status of the girl in v. 28-29.

The meaning of the word בְתוּלָה in this law and in the parallel Ex 22:15-16 is disputed (see above, pp. 25-28). The law requires the man who violates a girl to pay money to the father of the girl whom he has violated. Presumably the money is compensation for the loss of the bridewealth which the father would otherwise receive. The loss of the bridewealth is explicable in terms of the girl's loss of virginity. Had she not been virgin, it would be difficult to understand what damages her father would have sustained by her further violation. It is most likely that בְתוּלָה denotes her virginity.

44   Weinfeld, *DDS*, 284-288.

Those who argue that the passages treat two different cases[45] interpret Ex 22:15-16 as having to do with the seduction of a virgin and Deut 22:28-29 as having to do with rape.[46] The two passages employ different verbs. Ex 22:15-16 uses the *piel* of פתה to describe the man's behavior to the girl. Deut 22:28-29 uses the verb תפש. This position holds that פתה denotes seduction, while תפש implies the man's use of force. We accept that the two verbs do have the different meanings of seduction and coercion, but will argue that the difference is legally immaterial. The girl's consent or lack of consent is not a factor which defines the case.

The range of the verb פתה includes deception, persuasion, allurement and seduction; it does not, however, denote force. We may accept the customary interpretation of Ex 22:15-16 as a case of seduction.[47] The word תפש is more disputed. Weinfeld, for example, argues that the verb "means 'held' and not necessarily 'attacked.'"[48] Weinfeld overlooks the

---

45    von Rad, *Deuteronomy*, 143; Craigie, *Deuteronomy*, 295; Driver, *Deuteronomy*, 258.

46    We are using the word "rape" to refer to sexual intercourse with an unconsenting woman. It is clear, however, that the view of forcible violation found within the Deuteronomic family laws differs from the view of forcible violation held by contemporary American legislation in some essential ways.

      In our legal system, the offense is against the woman; the essence of the crime is the fact that the woman has not consented to the sexual act. In the Deuteronomic family laws, the offense is seen first of all as a violation of the claims of the man who controls the woman's sexuality. The essence of the offense is that the man's claims have been violated. The seriousness of the crime is determined by the nature of the man's claims. Sexual intercourse with a married or betrothed woman is a capital offense whether or not the woman has consented. Sexual intercourse with an unbetrothed girl is a minor offense whether or not the girl has consented. The woman's consent or lack of consent comes into play in determining whether she, as well as the male offender, is guilty of the violation of the claims of her husband, prospective husband, or father.

47    There is no text in the Hebrew Bible which suggests that the verb פתה denotes physical force.

48    Weinfeld, *DDS*, 286. Weinfeld cites Jer 40:10, וּשְׁבוּ בְּעָרֵיכֶם אֲשֶׁר־תְּפַשְׂתֶּם, "and live in towns that you have held," as an example to demonstrate his point. Towns are inanimate objects; it is more important for our study to examine the meaning of the verb when a human being is its object.

      Weinfeld also points to the verbal form וְנִמְצְאוּ "and they were found" as an indication of the culpability of both the man and the girl. The word וְנִמְצְאוּ is textually uncertain. Weinfeld notes that the LXX uses a singular ("and he is found") but ascribes the difference to the translator's assumption that the law concerns rape. The difference is more likely a matter of either dittography or haplography (the word is followed by a *waw*) MT: וְנִמְצְאוּ וְנָתַן. The use of the plural form in the SamP may make haplography the more likely explanation. Nonetheless, the text is too uncertain to be used as evidence that the girl has consented. Nor, given the varying ways in which מצא is used in Deut 22:13-29, would the plural form of the verb necessarily imply the girl's complicity. See Ceresko, "The Function of *Antanaclasis*," 551-569.

      Weinfeld, *DDS*, 286 n. 5, rightly notes that the explanatory clause תַּחַת אֲשֶׁר עִנָּה

fact that the meaning of the verb when its object is inanimate differs from its meaning with a human object. תפש ("lay hold of") may be used to refer to "holding" or even "handling skillfully" inanimate objects or cities. When the object of the verb is a human being, however, תפש has to do with involuntary seizure.[49]

Ex 22:15-16 does suggest that the girl has been seduced while Deut 22:28-29 suggests that she was coerced. The language describing the man's action in the Deuteronomic law ("If a man overtakes ... takes hold of and lies with") expresses an element of force not found in the Exodus text ("If a man seduces").

The question remains whether the force implied by the language of Deut 22:28 is a material factor in the case. Does the contrast between the language of seduction in Ex 22:15-16 and the language of force in Deut 22:28-29 mean that the two passages deal with two different cases? There are two reasons to argue that the girl's consent is not a material factor in the case.[50]

---

cannot be taken as evidence that the law refers to rape. The same verb, ענה, is used in 22:24, where the woman has clearly consented. It therefore cannot imply the man's use of force in the Deuteronomic laws. His interpretation of the verb is incorrect, however. Weinfeld holds that the verb refers to sexual intercourse in general and ought to be so translated in Gen 34:2; Judg 19:24; 2 Sam 13:12; Ez 22:10-11 and here. The verb does not refer to sexual intercourse in general. ענה is never used to express sexual intercourse which takes place in a socially accepted context. With the possible exception of Deut 21:14, the verb when used in reference to sexual intercourse has to do with illegal or violent actions.

49    The verb תפש is used with a human being as its direct object thirty-two times in biblical Hebrew. Of these instances, only once (Ez 29:7) is the verb to be understood in a benevolent sense of "grasping for support," and once in a context which leaves it ambiguous whether the person was forcibly seized. In all other cases, the verb refers to such actions as capture, seizure in battle, ensnarement, entrapment and arrest.
      The language of the Deuteronomic law seems to indicate that the girl has not consented to the sexual act. The man's action is described in v. 23 with the verbs מצא ושכב, and in v. 25 with the verbs מצא, חזק, and שכב. The man's action in v. 28 is described by the verbs מצא, תפש, and שכב. The similarity of the phrasing indicates that differences in wording are significant. The drafters want to distinguish the man's action in v. 28 from both forcible rape of a resisting girl in v. 25 and from the seduction of a consenting girl in v. 23.
      According to Driver and Miles, *AL*, 54-55, 494, the Middle Assyrian parallel to this law (MAL A:55-56, *ANET*, 185) also uses phrasing (*kî da'āni*) which indicates force or constraint, but which differs from the language used to express the violation of an unconsenting married woman (MAL A:12, *ANET*, 181). The phrasing in MAL A:12 uses an adverbial phrase (*emūqa*) which expresses force more unequivocally and adds the phrase "she ... strenuously defends herself."

50    This is in contrast to MAL A:55-56, *ANET*, 185, where marriage is imposed only if the girl did not consent. If she "gave herself to the man," the man is not required to marry her and her father may deal with her as he wishes.

First, if the redactor of this passage had wanted to distinguish between the case of an unbetrothed girl who consents to sexual relationships and an unbetrothed girl who resists, he would have included the alternate case as he did in v. 23-27, and as the drafters of the Middle Assyrian laws did in paragraphs 55 (concerning an unconsenting girl) and 56 (concerning a girl who consents).[51]

Second, the penalties imposed in Ex 22:15-16 and in Deut 22:28-29 are essentially the same. Both texts require that the man who violates the unbetrothed girl make a payment to her father and marry the girl. There are three differences between the apodosis of the two texts. Ex 22:16 refers to the payment as the bridewealth of virgins (מֹהַר הַבְּתוּלֹת) while Deut 22:28-29 mandates that the violator is to pay fifty shekels to the girl's father. Ex 22:16 explicitly allows the father to withhold his daughter from her seducer if he chooses to do so; the Deuteronomic law does not include such a caveat. Moreover, the Deuteronomic version of the law prohibits the violator from ever divorcing the girl; the Exodus version does not.

These differences, however, should not be exaggerated. Moreover, they do not appear to correlate with the difference between seduction and rape. The fifty shekels to be paid to the father according to Deut 22:29 is best understood as the equivalent of the "bridewealth of virgins" referred to in Ex 22:16. The phrase used in the Exodus passage "bridewealth of virgins" suggests a fixed, customary sum. Moreover, it is common for ancient Near Eastern laws to fix the price to be paid as compensation.[52] The difference in the two texts over whether the father is allowed to withhold his daughter from her violator is not likely to reflect the lawgivers' different appraisals of the case of seduction of a consenting girl and violation of an unconsenting girl. As Weinfeld has rightly argued, it is not likely that the father would have the right to withhold his daughter from a man who had seduced her, but would not be able to withhold her from a man who had raped her.[53] The Deuteronomic limitation of the man's right to divorce his wife might be intended to protect the injured girl.[54]

---

51    The Deuteronomic draftsman did not have to include the case of adultery with an unconsenting married woman in v. 22, because the laws have established that betrothed and married women are to be treated alike in respect to adultery. Therefore, one could determine how to treat a case involving an unconsenting married woman from v. 25-27. The cases of sexual relations with betrothed and unbetrothed girls are not to be treated alike, however, so one could not deduce how a consenting unbetrothed girl should be treated from v. 23.

52    See Westbrook, *SBCL*, 64-70.

53    Weinfeld, *DDS*, 287.

54    The Deuteronomic limitation of the man's right to divorce his injured wife may reflect an increase in the likelihood of divorce in the Deuteronomic period. According to Reuven Yaron, "On Divorce in Old Testament Times," *Revue*

Ex 22:15-16 and Deut 22:28-29 should be interpreted as variants of
the same case; that is, the violation of an unbetrothed girl. Weinfeld has
argued that the differences between the two variants reflect the
Deuteronomic redactors' humanitarian concern for the woman. His
argument cannot be sustained. Weinfeld argues that the father's
discretion over the marriage of his daughter to her violator in the Exodus
version of the law makes the girl more vulnerable. "It need hardly be said
that in such cases the continued presence of the maiden in her father's
household may well have heightened her shame and ruined her future
marriage prospects."[55] He interprets the fact that the Deuteronomic law
does not explicitly give the father discretion over the marriage of his
daughter to her violator as a reflection of the Deuteronomist's
humanitarian concern for the girl. It must be questioned, however,
whether the absence of the clause giving the father discretion in the
Deuteronomic text means that the Deuteronomic redactors intended to
exclude the father's right to withhold his daughter. It is possible that such
a right was assumed.

Similarly, Weinfeld wants to distinguish between the stipulation in the
Exodus law that the violator pay the *mohar* to the girl's father, and the
requirement in the Deuteronomic law that the violator give the father
fifty shekels. He understands the money paid to the father in Ex 22:16 as
compensation for the economic loss to the father caused by the fact that
his daughter is no longer a virgin and he will no longer be able to collect
bridewealth for her. Weinfeld sees the money paid to the father in
Deuteronomy as a fine unrelated to the bridewealth. He bases this
argument on the fact that the term *mohar* is not used in the
Deuteronomic text, and on the fact a fixed sum is given. The word *mohar*
is very rare in the Hebrew Bible, however; apart from the law in Exodus,
it occurs only in Gen 34:12 and 1 Sam 18:25. There are other passages
which involve bridewealth where the term is not used. The absence of the
term in Deut 22:29 is not surprising. Nor does the fact a specific sum was
mentioned mean the money is a fine rather than compensation. Fixed
price penalties are not unusual in ancient Near Eastern law. In both
Deuteronomy and Exodus, the father receives compensation for the
economic injury which his daughter's loss of virginity would cause him.

The Deuteronomic limitation of the violator's right to divorce his wife
may reflect the redactors' intention to protect the social and economic

---

*Internationale des droits de l'Antiquité* 4 (1957): 117-128; and Phyllis Bird, "Images of
Women in the Old Testament," in *Religion and Sexism: Images of Woman in the
Jewish and Christian Traditions*, ed. Rosemary Radford Ruether (New York: Simon
and Schuster, 1974), 53, all of the biblical references to formal divorce are
comparatively late. Such a limitation may not have been necessary at the time that
the Book of the Covenant was compiled.

55    Weinfeld, *DDS*, 285.

status of the violated girl. It may, however, reflect the increased frequency of divorce in the Deuteronomic period.

The law seems to reflect three concerns. First, the overall concern of Deut 22:13-29 seems to be to define what cases are to be considered adultery and thus subject to the death penalty. The inclusion of Deut 22:28-29 in this series of laws makes it clear that sexual intercourse with an unbetrothed girl is not considered adultery. Such clarification may have been necessary since Deut 22:20-21 makes a girl's entering into a marriage without her virginity intact an offense punishable by death.[56] Second, the law provides for the father to be compensated for the loss of the bridewealth. Third, the violator is required to marry the girl and is denied the right to divorce her. This provides security for the girl who having lost her virginity might otherwise be ineligible for marriage. It also serves the interests of the girl's father, since he does not have to provide for an unmarriageable daughter.[57]

### 3. The Purpose of the Passage as a Whole

The ordering of the passage places the law against slander at the beginning of a series of laws concerning sexual offenses. Laws against slander are (as Finkelstein notes) a common "topos" in ancient Near Eastern sexual offense laws. Finkelstein understands them as designed to show the lawgiver's concern for justice.[58] Placed at the beginning of laws concerning adultery, the law does seem aimed in part at protecting the girl from irresponsible accusations. It also protects her father and his household from dishonor. Phillips has raised the possibility that the law

---

56    The Deuteronomic placement of the law concerning sexual relations with an unbetrothed girl with sexual offense laws is different from the placement of the law in the Book of the Covenant where it is associated with laws having to do with financial compensation, or the parallel law in the MAL code, where it is associated with laws having to do with violence.

57    The rule that the man marry the girl he has violated is seen as a positive provision for the girl and not only for her father. This is shown by Tamar's response to Amnon's rejection (2 Sam 13:16). The Hebrew text is problematic at this verse, but it does indicate Tamar views Amnon's failure to marry her after having violated her as a great wrong. It is worth noting, however, that MAL A:55, *ANET*, 185, which similarly provides for the marriage of a violated girl to her violator also gives the girl's father the talion right to violate the wife of the seducer. Even if this last stipulation is only "a piece of 'calculated frightfulness'" (Finkelstein, "Sex Offenses," 357), it illustrates the MAL drafter's view of women as the property of their men, and shows that the rule that violators must provide a home for the women they have violated does not necessarily emerge from a strong regard for the needs of the women. Mandating marriage between a rapist and his victim is a not uncommon societal response to the problem of providing for a girl who has been rendered ineligible for marriage.

58    Finkelstein, "Sex Offenses," 367.

also limits the liability of the slanderer who might otherwise be accused
of giving false testimony and penalized according to Deut 19:16-19.[59]

The remaining cases (Deut 22:20-29) define what sexual offenses are
considered adulterous (non-virginity at marriage and sexual relations with
married or betrothed women, but not sexual relations with unbetrothed
women) and who is guilty of the offense.

The severity of the offense is emphasized by the penalty (death), the
repeated expurgation formula (v. 21, 22, and 24), and the great care taken
to determine who is or is not guilty. That adultery is seen as a grave
violation of the communal order as well as an offense against the husband
or father is indicated by the expurgation formula. The adulterers--both
male and female--must be killed in order to remove the evil from the
community and restore its purity. It is especially indicated by the
description of the unchaste bride's crime as a נְבָלָה בְּיִשְׂרָאֵל. This
emphasis on the community is in keeping with the Deuteronomic concern
for "Israel" and for the purity of Israel, and the Deuteronomic insistence
that all members of Israel are responsible for actualizing God's blessing
by obeying the law.

The Deuteronomic understanding of adultery as an offense against
the community, however, does not mean that the Deuteronomic authors
did not regard adultery as a violation of the rights of the husband or the
father. Rather, it is precisely as a violation of the husband's or father's
rights that adultery was perceived as a serious threat to the social order.
This is explicit in the wording of 22:21. The unchaste bride has done a
gravely disorderly thing in Israel, to engage in sexual relations while
under the authority of her father.

Overall, the passage stresses the prohibition against adultery as
important to the stability of the family which in turn is foundational to the
society. This interpretation of the laws, however, is accurate only if one
explicitly recognizes that the Deuteronomic (and ancient Near Eastern)
laws understood family stability or family morality in terms of the
interests and rights of the father and husband. The laws prohibiting
adultery recognize the rights of the father to exclusive disposal of his
daughter's sexuality and especially the rights of the husband to exclusive
possession of his wife's sexuality. The wife has no such reciprocal claim.

This asymmetry shows that the issue was not protection of intimacy in
marriage, or of chastity, per se. Rather, what was at stake in the laws
concerning adultery was the authority of the male head of the household.
This in turn was likely to have been a matter of paternity--the imperative
need, in a patrilineal society, for a father to be certain that his sons were
his own.

---

59    See p. 24-25.

Inclusive descriptions of the concern of these laws as "the protection of marriage" or "family morality" obscure the particular orientation of the ancient Near Eastern view of the family, a view thoroughly shared by the Deuteronomic legislation.

The laws also protect the wife from false accusations, and provide for the socially vulnerable girl (22:28-29). It is not possible to distinguish completely in these cases the extent to which the laws protect the girl, and the extent to which they protect her father.

### 4. *The Social and Familial Patterns Assumed by the Laws*

The passage shows clearly that in terms of her sexuality at least, the unmarried girl was under her father's authority, as the married woman was under the authority of her husband.

That women are the object, not the subject, of marriage arrangements is widely recognized. They are clearly the object rather than the subject of these laws. Grammatically, the woman, as object, is taken, entered, spurned, given, and overtaken. She is found, as subject, in explanatory clauses, in the phrase "She shall be his wife," and in judgments: "She has committed a sacrilege in Israel," "She shall die."

Legally, the woman's status is determined by her relationship (or non-relationship) to a man. As Phyllis Bird has noted, whether a woman's actions toward a man and whether a man's actions toward a woman are offenses or not is determined by whether the woman has obligations to a husband, father, or father-in-law.[60]

The laws appear to be addressed to men, rather than to women. (The plural "you" in v. 24 may be identified with the "men of her town" in v. 21.)

The woman is not entirely without legal standing. She is liable to the law (whether this is a Deuteronomic innovation will be explored in another chapter). She can, with her husband, be a plaintiff before the elders.

---

60    See Bird, "To Play the Harlot," 77.

# Chapter Three: The Prohibition against
## the Restoration of Marriage: Deuteronomy 24:1-4

## 1. *Introduction*

Deut 24:1-4 has been the subject of intense scholarly debate.[1] Contemporary biblical scholars generally agree about the meaning of the passage at the most literal level: it prohibits the remarriage of a man to a woman whom he has previously divorced, if the woman has in the meantime contracted a second marriage.

The rationale underlying the law, however, is not self-evident. Both the first and second marriages were legally contracted and legally terminated. No man's rights have been violated. It is not clear that any illicit behavior has taken place. Why then is the woman defiled in relationship to her first husband? Why is he forbidden to marry her? The rationale of the law is more difficult to discern because it has no known parallel in either the Bible or in the cuneiform texts.[2]

Attempts to explain the rationale have varied widely. Scholars have posited that the law was intended to deter divorce and thus protect the first marriage, that it was designed to protect the woman's second marriage, or, most recently, that it was intended to prevent the first husband from economically exploiting his former wife. Some suppose that the law regards the remarriage of a divorced couple as incestuous; others, that the woman was understood to have been guilty of sexual misconduct during her first marriage.[3]

---

1   Deut 24:1-4 contains the only biblical law which provides details concerning the dissolution of a marriage; it therefore became the basis for rabbinical law about divorce. As such, it has been the subject of intense study and debate. The debate of the rabbis (and of much subsequent scholarship) centered on the meaning of the phrase עֶרְוַת דָּבָר "some indecency" in v. 1, which was understood to define the grounds upon which a man could be allowed to divorce his wife.

   The meaning of the term is still widely disputed (see p. 57 n. 44). There is, however, a near consensus among contemporary scholars that the passage in its received form does not include a general law of divorce, and thus does not set the grounds for divorce. The dispute over the phrase, while still significant for interpreting the law, carries correspondingly less weight.

2   Gen 20:1-18 and 2 Sam 3:12-16 are frequently cited in relationship to Deut 24:1-4, usually to suggest that the law against palingamy was not effective in the early period of Israel's history. Neither Abraham's restored relationship with Sarah after she was with Abimelech, nor the relationship between David and Michal is comparable to the situation envisioned in Deut 24:1-4, however, because neither Abraham nor David had divorced his wife.

3   These positions are discussed below, pp. 51-59.

The position argued here interprets the law in terms of sexual impurity. Specifically, following Craigie and Miller,[4] it interprets the restored marriage as analogous to adultery. Like adultery, the relationship which the law prohibits would involve a woman having sexual relations first with man A, then with man B, then again with man A. The significance of the law, according to this interpretation, is that it suggests the Deuteronomic view of proper or improper sexual conduct was not defined exclusively in terms of men's legal rights. Rather, the Deuteronomic concern for purity and for the integrity of the family transcends and can even limit male prerogative.

The widely divergent ways in which this passage has been understood make it particularly important to clarify the bases upon which one interprets the passage. An explanation of the law must take into account three elements: (1) the structure of the law, (2) the multiple conditions which comprise the protasis of the law, and (3) the motive clauses found in v. 4. Our discussion of Deut 24:1-4 will begin by examining those three elements. The second part of the discussion will argue that most of the interpretations of the law fail to take into account one of these three elements. Westbrook's recent interpretation of the law constitutes the most serious challenge to our view; the third part of this discussion will examine and refute Westbrook's position in some detail. Finally, we will suggest that the relationship prohibited by the law should be seen as analogous to adultery, and understood in terms of sexual purity and pollution.

### 2. Deuteronomy 24:1-4: Bases for Interpretation

#### a. Structure

There is near consensus among contemporary scholars that the protasis of the law continues through the first three verses of the passage. The apodosis comes only in v. 4, with the words לֹא־יוּכַל.

The early rabbis, the early church, and many subsequent interpreters of the passage held that v. 1 contained both protasis and apodosis: "If a man takes a wife and marries her and she finds no favor in his eyes because he has found some indecency in her, then he shall write her a bill of divorcement and put it in her hand and send her out of his house."[5]

If v. 1 stood alone, such an interpretation would be plausible. Within the first three verses, however, there is a series of ten perfect verbs each preceded by a *waw*. There is no formal reason to interpret some of these ten verbs as belonging to the protasis and some of them as a subclause

---

4    Craigie, *Deuteronomy*, 304-306; Miller, *Deuteronomy*, 164.
5    The American Standard Version of the Bible (New York: Thomas Nelson & Sons, 1929), also translates v. 1 as containing both protasis and apodosis.

forming an apodosis. Similarly, there is no reason to translate the phrase "and he writes her a bill of divorcement and puts it in her hand" differently in v. 1 and v. 3. Moreover, there is no particle to introduce a sub-case.[6] The clauses in the protasis (v. 1-3) define the specific conditions under which the prohibition of v. 4 becomes operative.

### b. *Conditions*

The protasis of the law (v. 1-3) includes four parts:
1. A man marries a woman.
2. He divorces her because he has found some indecency in her.
3. She becomes the wife of another man.
4. The other man either divorces her because he dislikes her, or he dies.

These four clauses define the specific conditions under which the prohibition against the first husband remarrying his former wife will come into effect. The complexity of the protasis of the law accounts in part for the lack of any consensus around its rationale. It also serves as a criterion for evaluating the various proposed interpretations. Presumably all of the explicit conditions given in the protasis are legally meaningful; an adequate interpretation of the rationale of the passage must take all four conditions into account.[7]

---

6    Mayes, *Deuteronomy*, 322, moreover, correctly argues that the law includes none of the financial matters which are invariably included in the cuneiform laws concerning divorce, and which one would expect in Deut 24:1-4 if the law intended to include a general law of divorce in v. 1.

7    Westbrook makes accounting for the various conditions in the protasis the key criterion by which he evaluates any interpretation of the law. He finds that all explanations except his own fail to account for one or more of the clauses in the protasis. See Raymond Westbrook, "The Prohibition of Restoration of Marriage in Deuteronomy 24:1-4," in *Studies in Bible*, Scripta Hierosolymitana 31 (Jerusalem: Magnes Press, 1986), 385-405.

Yaron, *Laws of Eshnunna*, 91, takes the opposite view. He believes that since many of the laws in the cuneiform codes are based on actual cases, the protasis will often consist of a recital of the facts in the actual case, and that not all of those facts are legally material. Yaron cites several examples of conditions included in the protases of the laws of Eshnunna which he considers immaterial.

Yaron overstates his case. It may not be necessary for each of the specific conditions included in the protasis of a law to be present before the apodosis goes into effect. For example, a father who arbitrarily broke a betrothal agreement would probably have to pay a penalty to the erstwhile groom whether he gave his daughter to another man or not. The concrete details of the clause "and gave his daughter to another man," are not necessary conditions for the law to come into effect. The clause does, however, play a role in one's understanding of the protasis. That is, it establishes that the father broke the betrothal agreement arbitrarily, without grounds. The arbitrariness of the father's action is a necessary condition for the law to go into effect.

c. *Motive Clauses*

The law does not provide a penalty; it seeks to bring about compliance by three motivational clauses.

1. She has defiled herself/been declared defiled.
2. It is an abomination before Yahweh.
3. You shall not cause the land which Yahweh your God is giving you as an inheritance to incur guilt.

The first motive clause, אַחֲרֵי אֲשֶׁר הֻטַּמָּאָה, "after she has been made (or declared) defiled," is explanatory. It is widely and correctly understood in terms of sexual defilement. There are several instances in the Hebrew Bible where a woman is said to have been defiled or to have defiled herself.[8] In each case, uncleanness is a result of illicit sexual intercourse: adultery (Num 5; Ez 18:6), harlotry (Hos 5:3; Ez 23:17), incest (Ez 22:10-11), or rape or seduction (Gen 34:27). The passage does not restrict marriage between the woman and a third husband. Rather, apparently she has been defiled only in relationship to her former husband.[9]

----

Moreover, Deut 24:1-4 spends far too many words establishing that the woman has been married a second time for that fact to be immaterial. Also, it considers two possible ways in which the second marriage might end: through divorce or death of the husband. Since two alternatives for the dissolution of the second marriage are given, the draftsman is obviously not simply listing the facts of an actual case, but rather intends for both to be taken into account.

8    Women, like men, are also rendered unclean by corpse contamination, by bodily emissions, and by skin disease. This kind of defilement, however, is of a different category from the kind of defilement which results from illicit sexuality. The former kinds of uncleanness last for a set period of time, are contagious, and seem to have no moral connotations. The latter, like the defilement which results from idolatry or bloodshed, is permanent, and has to do with divine sanction against wrongdoing. Our law has to do with this second kind of pollution beliefs. See Tikva Frymer-Kensky, "Pollution, Purification, and Purgation in Biblical Israel," in *The Word of the Lord Shall Go Forth*, ed. C. Meyers and M. O'Connor, (Winona Lake, Ind.: Eisenbrauns, 1983), 399-414.

9    Westbrook, "Restoration of Marriage," 404-405, has noted that the mood of the consonantal form of the verbהטמאה could be taken in a declarative passive sense.

Westbrook is correct that the verbal form is ambiguous. The verb is usually identified on the basis of the MT pointing as a "*hothpa'al*" (e.g., GKC 54.3), which is taken to be the passive of the reflexive. The "*hothpa'al*" is, however, a questionable form. It is found in only two other places: Lev 13:55-56 (הֻכַּבֵּס) and Is 34:6 (הֻדַּשְׁנָה). There is no ת found in any of these three examples of the "*hothpa'al*" form (the ת is assumed to have been assimilated). This means that the evidence for the existence of such a form is dependent on the MT pointing rather than the consonantal text.

Charles Torrey, *The Second Isaiah* (New York: Charles Scribners, 1928), 284, has suggested plausibly that the origin of the pointing was to show that there were two alternative readings of the verbs: *hophal* or *hithpael*. Taken as a *hophal*, the verb could be rendered as either a causative passive or a declarative passive: "she has

The second motive clause, כִּי־תוֹעֵבָה הִוא לִפְנֵי יְהוָה, "it is an abomination before Yahweh,"[10] is a variation of a clause which is repeated in conjunction with a number of Deuteronomic laws. Scholars often assert that the Deuteronomic authors associated the word תּוֹעֵבָה, "abomination," with Canaanite cultic practices.[11] In fact, the word תּוֹעֵבָה is associated with two different kinds of laws. One group of passages indeed uses תּוֹעֵבָה in reference to the religious practices of the nations. Idolatry, child Molech service, and other mantic practices are תּוֹעֵב ת which the other nations practice and which threaten the purity of Yahwism.[12] The תּוֹעֵב ת are said to be the reason that God has driven the nations out before Israel. They, or those doing them, are subject to destruction.

The word תּוֹעֵבָה, however, is used in connection with other laws which do not appear to be directly related to Canaanite practices. Deut 17:1 calls sacrificing a blemished ox or sheep "an abomination to the Lord your God." Israel is commanded not to eat any abominable thing (Deut 14:3). For a man or a woman to wear the garments of a member of the opposite sex is an "abomination to the Lord your God" (Deut 22:5). Prostitution by men or women, and especially using money earned by prostitution to pay a vow is also תּוֹעֲבַת יְהוָה (Deut 23:19). These laws have all been described as prohibiting Canaanite practices. This interpretation seems, however, to be governed by the assumption that anything described as תּוֹעֵבָה is necessarily Canaanite.[13] In fact, these laws

---

been defiled" or "she has been declared defiled." A causative or declarative translation of the verb finds some support in Targum Onkelos, where the verb is translated דְּאִסְתָּאֲבַת. The *ithpaal* of סאב can mean "to be made or declared unclean" as well as "to be unclean." The meaning of the *hithpael* of טמא is reflexive: "to defile oneself" (*BDB*, 379).

　　Whether the verb should be translated in a declarative or a causative sense must be decided on exegetical rather than grammatical grounds. I will argue below that Westbrook's interpretation of the passage, which requires translating the verb "declared defiled," cannot finally be sustained, and will therefore take the verb to mean "has been defiled."

10　The pointing of the pronoun is feminine: כִּי־תוֹעֵבָה הִוא. It would be possible to translate the phrase: "she is an abomination." The phrase appears again at Gen 43:32, and without the particle כִּי at Lev 18:22, where the pronoun must be translated "it." It is best to understand the phrase as referring to the act of remarriage rather than to the woman.

11　See for example Jean L'Hour, "Les Interdits *To'eba* dans le Deuteronome," *Revue Biblique* 71 (1964): 481-503; Paul Humbert, "Le Substantif *to'eba* et le verbe *t'b* dans l'Ancien Testament," *ZAW* 72 (1960): 217-237, and most commentators.

12　Idolatry: Deut 7:25; 13:15; 17:4; 20:18; 27:15; child Molech service: 12:31; 18:10; other mantic practices: 18:9-12.

13　Wearing the clothing of the opposite sex, for example, is supposed to have been a part of foreign cultic rituals. Such cultic practices are not attested prior to the Hellenistic period, however; see Richard Clifford, *Deuteronomy With an Excursus on Covenant and Law*, Old Testament Message (Wilmington, Delaware: Michael Glazier, Inc., 1989), 117. Similarly, many scholars assume that the prostitute referred

have to do with purity. Only a pure animal may be sacrificed; only clean food may be eaten. One may not bring to the temple what Craigie calls "dirty money."[14] The law against wearing the garments of the opposite sex also has to do with purity. One aspect of the biblical concept of purity has to do with keeping the categories of existence properly separated.[15] Mixing things which should not be mixed violates the purity of the community.[16]

The theme common to all of the laws using תּוֹעֵבָה is the concept of purity. One set of laws has to do with the purity of Yahwism in opposition to syncretism; the second set concerns the purity of Israel's life and cult.[17] The presence of the motive clause "it is an abomination before Yahweh" in Deut 24:1-4 suggests that the law has to do with the purity of Israel.[18]

The final motive clause, "You shall not cause the land which Yahweh your God is giving you as an inheritance to incur guilt,"[19] also categorizes the prohibited remarriage as polluting.[20] The concept that sin defiles the

---

to in 23:19 is associated with the cult. They reason that the זוֹנָה is the same as the קְדֵשָׁה of 23:18, which they take to mean "cult prostitute." Recent scholarship has cast serious doubts on the view that the קְדֵשָׁה was a cult prostitute, however; see Bird, "To Play the Harlot," n. 1 for references. Moreover, equating the קְדֵשָׁה and זוֹנָה makes v. 19 redundant. It would be superfluous for v. 19 to rule out bringing the pay of a class of persons to the temple if that class of persons had no legal right to exist. It is best to interpret v. 19 as referring to commercial prostitution rather than to cultic or Canaanite practices. Nor is there any compelling reason to understand the sacrifice of blemished animals or consumption of unclean foods in relationship to Canaanite practices.

14  Craigie, *Deuteronomy*, 301.

15  See Miller, *Deuteronomy*, 162.

16  Cf. Deut 22:9-11. Cf. also Lev 18:23, where the unclean practice of bestiality is called תֶּבֶל, "confusion."

17  "It is an abomination" is found as the motive clause for one law having to do with social justice; that is, the prohibition against using false weights and measures. This exception may be explained in terms of the history of the prohibition. The use of false weights and balances is called an "abomination" three different times in the book of Proverbs (16:11-12; 20:10; 20:23). The Deuteronomic redactors may have simply included the assertion that false weights were an "abomination" when they incorporated the prohibition into their laws.

18  See Henri Cazelles, "Pureté et Impureté, Ancien Testament," *DBS*, 497.

19  This meaning for the *hiphil* of חטא is found in Is 29:21 and probably Qoh 5:5.

20  Deut 24:4 uses the *hiphil* stem of חטא, while the biblical references to the pollution of the land use טמא, חלל, זנה, or חנף. This difference should not, however, be overdrawn. Weinfeld overemphasizes the distinction between sin lying on the people and the defilement of the land, "On 'Demythologization and Secularization' in Deuteronomy," *Israel Exploration Journal* 23 (1973): 232. There is considerable semantic overlap between חטא and טמא (see Lam 1:8-9; Ez 37:23; Is 64:4-5 [Eng. 64:5-6]). Sin leads to defilement; the very land itself may be polluted by the sin of its inhabitants.

That Deut 24:4 has to do with polluting the land is confirmed by the close resemblance between 24:4c and Deut 21:23:

very land and brings catastrophe upon it is not uncommon in the Hebrew Bible. The kinds of sin which are said to pollute the land consistently fall into three categories. Apostasy pollutes the land.[21] Bloodguilt pollutes the land.[22] And finally, sexual defilement pollutes the land.[23] The third motive clause thus implies that the restored marriage would be a sexual offense which would pollute the land.

Taken together, the three motive clauses indicate that Deut 24:1-4 is concerned with purity and pollution; the restored marriage is viewed as an offense against sexual purity.[24]

### 3. Implausible Interpretations of Deuteronomy 24:1-4

An adequate interpretation of Deut 24:1-4 should account for the structure of the law, each of the conditions contained in the protasis of the law, and the motive clauses. Most interpretations fail to provide for one or more of these elements.

Driver holds that Deut 24:1-4 was intended to prevent hasty or ill-considered divorce. He finds four deterrents in the passage. (1) He takes עֶרְוַת דָּבָר to mean that the man divorcing his wife would have to have clear grounds. (2) The law refers to a "bill of divorcement"; Driver believes that it mandates preparing such a legal instrument in order to deter impulsive divorce. (3) Because he understands the law as requiring the husband to show cause for divorce, he believes it implicitly requires that divorce take place before an official who could evaluate the reasons for the husband's actions. (4) Finally, Driver suggests that the prohibition against remarriage after the wife has been married to another man would act as a deterrent by making it clear that the divorce was final.[25]

---

| Deut 24:4 | וְלֹא תַחֲטִיא אֶת־הָאָרֶץ |
| | אֲשֶׁר יְהוָה אֱלֹהֶיךָ נֹתֵן לְךָ נַחֲלָה |
| Deut 21:23 | וְלֹא תְטַמֵּא אֶת־אַדְמָתְךָ |
| | אֲשֶׁר יְהוָה אֱלֹהֶיךָ נֹתֵן לְךָ נַחֲלָה |

The verb used in Deut 21:23 (טמא) clearly belongs to the sphere of pollution.

Both Jer 3:1 and the LXX have interpreted Deut 24:4c as warning that the land would be defiled. The LXX reads *mianeîte*, "defile," while Jeremiah reads: הֲלוֹא חָנוֹף תֶּחֱנַף הָאָרֶץ הַהִיא, "Would not that land be truly defiled?"

21 Jer 2:7; 3:9; Ez 23:17, 30; 36:17-18; Ps 106:38.
22 Deut 21:22-23; Num 35:31-34; Ps 106:38.
23 Lev 18:24-30; Jer 3:1; taking adultery as a metaphor for idolatry, Ez 23:17; Jer 3:9. For further discussion of pollution and the land, see Frymer-Kensky, "Pollution, Purification, and Purgation," 406-409.
24 The concepts of defilement, abomination, and polluting the land are also found together in Lev 18:26-28, which is a paranetic summary of a series of laws prohibiting aberrant sexual practices.
25 Driver, *Deuteronomy*, 269-273.

Driver's interpretation disregards the structure of the law. That is, the statement that the man finds some indecency in the woman, and the statement that he writes for her a bill of divorce are part of the protasis, defining the conditions of the case, not part of what the law mandates.[26] Only Driver's fourth point, the prohibition against remarriage, actually belongs to the apodosis. It is, however, extremely unlikely that a law which wished to deter a man from hastily divorcing his wife would do so by prohibiting him from remarrying her some time later, should she happen to marry again, and should her second husband happen to die or decide also to divorce her. As Westbrook notes, the case is entirely too complicated for the purpose which Driver assigns to it.[27]

Wenham finds a rationale for the law in the incest taboos enumerated in Leviticus 18 and 20. He takes as his starting point the passage's three motive clauses, and the fact that defilement, abomination, and pollution of the land are also found as motive clauses for the sexual offense laws of Leviticus. Wenham argues that marriage creates a blood relationship between husband and wife. He demonstrates that relationships created by marriage are assumed by the levitical law to continue beyond the end of the marriage. The woman in the case had become her husband's closest relative when he first married her; that relationship would endure. According to Wenham, for a man to remarry his divorced wife would be to marry his closest relative. It would be incestuous in the same way that marrying one's sister would be incestuous.[28]

Wenham's interpretation is subject to criticism because it makes v. 2-3 irrelevant. The man's marriage to the woman would have made her a close relative, and remarriage would have thus been considered incestous, regardless of whether or or not the woman had contracted another marriage in the interim.[29] Wenham's interpretation does not do justice to the complexity of the law.

Yaron believes that the law was intended to protect the second marriage. Either the first husband or the wife could have regretted the initial divorce and intrigued against the second marriage in an attempt to restore the first marriage. Moreover, the second husband might have been jealous of the first husband whether or not such jealousy was justified. The law would prevent such disruption to the second marriage.[30]

Yaron's interpretation of the passage does take the second marriage into consideration. However, while his interpretation accounts for the

26    Deut 24:1-4 assumes that divorce takes place by the husband putting a bill of divorce into the hand of his wife.

27    Westbrook, "Restoration of Marriage," 389.

28    Gordon J. Wenham, "The Restoration of Marriage Reconsidered," *JJS* 30 (1979): 36-40.

29    So, Westbrook, "Restoration of Marriage," 390-391.

30    Reuven Yaron, "The Restoration of Marriage," *JJS* 17 (1966): 1-11.

prohibition against remarriage if the woman's second marriage ended in divorce, it does not explain why the remarriage was also prohibited if the woman's second husband died.[31]

Moreover, Yaron's interpretation is unable to account for the first motive clause. The first husband may not remarry his former wife after she has married another man because הֻטַּמָּאָה: she has been declared, or made, or is defiled. The defilement of the woman, whether alleged or actual, must play a role in the interpretation of the law.

Finally, Weinfeld believes that the woman was defiled because she engaged in illicit or aberrant sexual relations with the man who later became her second husband while she was married to her first husband.[32] He bases his interpretation on the phrases עֶרְוַת דָּבָר and הֻטַּמָּאָה.

There is nothing in the law, however, to connect the second marriage with the "indecency" which the woman's first husband had found in her. Nor is there anything to suggest that the second marriage was invalid or adulterous. Moreover, this kind of interpretation takes the phrase עֶרְוַת דָּבָר to refer to grave sexual misconduct, a possible but far from certain translation. Finally, it is difficult to understand why the woman's sexual misconduct would defile her in relationship to her first husband but not in relationship to any other man.

### 4. Westbrook's Interpretation

Westbrook has proposed an explanation of the rationale of Deut 24:1-4 which radically departs from previous interpretations of the passage. He believes that the law sought to prevent the first husband from economically exploiting the woman who may have acquired wealth through her second marriage.[33] Because Westbrook's interpretation is so different from any other explanation of the law, and because of the coherency of his view, we will examine and refute it in some detail.

---

31    Both Westbrook, "Restoration of Marriage," 390, and Wenham, "Restoration of Marriage Reconsidered," 37, make this point.

32    Weinfeld, *DDS*, 269 n. 4. Weinfeld is following a very old tradition of interpretation. Philo had already interpreted the woman as an adulteress because she entered into a second marriage in *Special Laws*, 3.3-31 (Loeb edition):

> She must not return to her first husband but ally herself with any other rather than him because she has broken with the rules that bound her in the past and cast them into oblivion when she chose new love-ties in preference to the old. And if a man is willing to contract himself with such a woman, he must be saddled with a character of degeneracy and loss of manhood ... and has taken upon him the stamp of two heinous crimes, adultery and pandering. For such subsequent reconciliations are proofs of both. The proper punishment for him is death and for the woman also.

33    Westbrook, "Restoration of Marriage," 404-405.

Westbrook's argument takes as its starting point "the difference in the dissolution of the first and second marriages."[34] The first husband is said to divorce his wife because he has found some indecency in her. The second marriage ends either because the husband dislikes his wife and divorces her, or because he dies. Westbrook takes the phrase כִּי־מָצָא בָה עֶרְוַת דָּבָר to mean that the first husband has claimed some objective fault in his wife as grounds for the divorce. He understands שְׂנֵאָה, on the other hand, as a technical term used to show that the second husband's action stemmed from his subjective decision and was not justified by any behavior or trait of the woman.[35]

Westbrook then notes that the financial consequences when the marriage ends through no fault of the woman (that is, if she is divorced without grounds, or if her husband dies) are drastically different from cases where the woman is found to be at fault in a divorce.

The Hebrew Bible provides no information about the monetary aspects of divorce or widowhood. Comparative ancient Near Eastern and Mishnaic materials, however, suggest that a woman who was divorced through no fault of her own was accorded at least her dowry and often an additional sum of divorce money.[36] Similarly, a woman who was widowed

---

34    Ibid., 393.

35    Both the Akkadian *zêru* and the Hebrew שׂנא are found by themselves to express the action "divorce." The Akkadian is found in an Old Babylonian marriage contract, CT 6 26a, translated by Westbrook in OBML, vol. 1, 111-112; the Hebrew is found in marriage contracts from Elephantine; see Yaron, *Aramaic Papyri*, 55. Westbrook convincingly argues that the terms are used in these documents as abbreviations of the fuller phrase "hate and divorce" (OMBL, vol. 2, 38).

36    The cuneiform and mishnaic evidence that women divorced through no fault of their own were provided at least some financial provisions is quite consistent. CU 6/7, *ANET*, 524, requires the man to pay one mina silver; CH 138-140, *ANET*, 172, sets the divorce money for a childless woman at an amount equal to the woman's bridewealth (*terhatum*), or if there had been no bridewealth fixes a sum of one or one-half minas, depending on the woman's status. The woman kept her dowry.

A marriage contract from Alalakh (no. 92) allows the husband to retain the bridewealth if his wife was at fault in divorce; see Isaac Mendelsohn, "On Marriage in Alalakh," in *Essays on Jewish Life and Thought*, ed. J. Blau et al. (New York: Columbia University Press, 1959), 352-353.

MAL A:29, *ANET*, 182, provides for the woman to keep her dowry, which is reserved for her sons. MAL A:38, *ANET*, 183, may say that the bridewealth of a woman dwelling in her father's house is reserved for the woman in case of divorce; the reading is disputed. See Driver and Miles, *AL*, 191-193, 405, 477; and Guillume Cardascia, *Les Lois Assyriennes*, (Paris: Les Editions du Cerf, 1969), 192-196. MAL A:37, *ANET*, 183, leaves it up to the husband to decide whether or not he will give anything to a wife whom he divorces; this law, however, must be read in light of MAL A:29. It most likely refers to divorce money coming from the husband's family, not to the dowry which the wife brought with her into the marriage.

Neo-Babylonian marriage contracts surveyed by Martha Roth, *Babylonian Marriage Agreements 7th - 3rd Centuries B.C.*, AOAT 222 (Neukirchen-Vluyn:

received at least her dowry, and often a settlement determined either by the husband at the time of marriage, or by the courts after his death.[37] A woman who was found to have been at fault in a divorce, however, received a smaller financial provision or none at all.[38]

According to Westbrook's interpretation of Deut 24:1-4, the first husband divorced his wife with cause, and thus would probably have kept the wife's dowry and would have been released from his obligation to pay her divorce money. The law envisions the woman contracting a second marriage which this time ends through no fault of hers. The woman in this case would have received certain properties from her second husband.

---

Neukirchener Verlag, 1989), 12-14, include penalty clauses which require the husband to pay from one to six minas of silver should he divorce his wife in order to marry another woman.

Three marriage contracts found at Elephantine include stipulations which acknowledge the right of either the husband or the wife to divorce his or her spouse, but which penalize the one who initiates the divorce a set amount. The woman keeps her dowry in either case. The amount of divorce money which the husband pays is variable; according to Yaron neither the *mohar* nor the divorce money is a large enough sum to represent a serious restraint on divorce, although the husband's obligation to return his wife's dowry may have deterred him from initiating divorce (*Aramaic Papyri*, 53-64).

37   CH 171-172, *ANET*, 173, accords a widow the usufruct of her dowry and her settlement (the *nudunnûm*). If her husband had not assigned her a settlement, she was to be given the usufruct of her deceased husband's estate equal to the share of one heir. She was not, however, allowed to take property from her husband's estate with her into a second marriage.

The MAL speak of a *nudunnûm* as well as other gifts from the husband to the wife (A:32, *ANET*, 182; A:27, *ANET*, 182; see also A:25, *ANET*, 182). They do not, unfortunately, provide any information about the case where the widow has not been assigned a settlement by her husband, nor do they indicate what would happen to the *nudunnûm* should the woman remarry.

NBL 12 accords the woman her dowry and a marriage gift; if the woman had no dowry, the law provides for the judicial authorities to assign her a portion of her husband's estate (Roth, *BMA*, 31-32). NBL 13 allows the woman to take the usufruct of the dowry and anything which her husband had assigned her with her into a second marriage (*ANET*, 197; Roth, *BMA*, 32-33).

38   According to Westbrook, CH 141 mandates that the husband of a woman found guilty of misconduct can divorce her without paying divorce money or journey money (OBML, vol. 2, 213). In the Alalakh contract cited above, the wife's family would lose the bridewealth if she were at fault. The Elephantine contracts penalized the spouse who initiated the divorce a set sum (Yaron, *Aramaic Papyri*, 53-64). The MAL evidence is uncertain. Cardascia, *Lois Assyriennes*, 159-164, believes that the last clause of A:29 allows a husband to keep his wife's dowry if he divorces her with cause; his interpretation of the key verb in the clause, however, is dependent upon comparative evidence rather than on philological evidence. Cardascia's interpretation therefore cannot be taken as evidence for the consistency of ancient Near Eastern practice. The Mishna rules that a woman who has transgressed the Law of Moses or Jewish custom can be divorced without repaying her *Ketubah* (m. Ketub, 7:6).

Westbrook believes that the prohibition in v. 4 is intended to prevent the first husband from seeking to remarry the woman in order to profit by the property she gained from her second marriage.

Westbrook understands v. 4b as the statement "she has been caused to be unclean" by her first husband's assertion that he had found some indecency in her.[39] The husband profited by declaring that she was unclean; he cannot reverse himself and marry her now that it would profit him to do so.[40]

### 5. Assessment of Westbrook's Position

Westbrook's interpretation is very attractive. He accounts for each of the conditions in the protasis. His evidence from the comparative material is particularly impressive in that he has traced patterns which span the range of cuneiform and Hebrew sources from Ur Nammu to the Mishna. Moreover, his interpretation fits the Deuteronomic context very well. The laws contained in Deut 24 mainly have to do with prohibiting exploitation of one's fellows or with generous treatment of those who are oppressed.[41] His argument is not finally persuasive, however, for three reasons.

First, Westbrook's interpretation of the distinction between לֹא מָצָא בָה עֶרְוַת דָּבָר כִּי־מָצָא בְעֵינָיו תִמְצָא־חֵן and שָׂנֵא is not convincing. His understanding of the meaning of שׂנא when it is used as a technical legal term is based primarily on his study of the verb's Akkadian counterpart, zêru. Westbrook cites four cases in the Code of Hammurabi in which he believes zêru, "hate," refers to the motivation for the act and is a necessary condition for the penalty (the *mens rea*).[42] That is, the person is penalized because his or her action was without objective grounds.

The one time the Code of Hammurabi uses the verb zêru in connection with divorce, however, is found in a case where an inchoately married woman who "hated" her betrothed husband and refused to marry him was determined by the local court to be blameless (CH 142). The

---

39 See p. 48 n. 9.

40 Westbrook, "Restoration of Marriage," 404-405.

41 This includes prohibitions against taking a millstone in pledge (v. 6); kidnapping a fellow-Israelite (v. 7); humanitarian prohibitions having to do with pledges (v. 10-13); payment of a poor person's wages (v. 14-15); prohibition against unjust treatment of vulnerable groups (v. 17-18); and the law of gleaning (v. 19-22).

42 The four cases include two concerning a man who hates and abandons his city (CE 30, *ANET*, 162; CH 136, *ANET*, 171); one in which a son hates and leaves his foster parents (CH 193, *ANET*, 175); and one where a woman hates her betrothed husband and refuses to complete the marriage, according to Westbrook's interpretation, OBML, vol. 2, 100-104, (CH 142, *ANET*, 172).

companion case, where the woman is found to be a gadabout and suffers the death penalty, does not use the term *zêru*.[43]

Furthermore, the contrast which Westbrook draws between מָצָא בָה עֶרְוַת דָּבָר and שָׂנֵאה can only be as certain as one's translation of עֶרְוַת דָּבָר. Few phrases in the Hebrew Bible have been more disputed. Westbrook seems to be correct when he suggests that the phrase "found in her" points to some objective characteristic or action of the woman; it is impossible to assess, however, the gravity of the "indecent thing" which evoked her husband's displeasure. It was certainly not something serious enough to disqualify the woman from entering into a second marriage.[44]

---

43    Westbrook writes: "The use of the verb 'to hate' even there is, we submit, an indication of the hostile attitude to the wife's action taken by the law ... CH is ruling on a case where the presumption of lack of justification was much stronger for a woman than for a man. Its purpose is to provide machinery whereby she can rebut the *prima facie* view of her action" (OBML, vol. 2, 228). His argument appears *ad hoc*.

Nor is Westbrook able to cite any cases which clearly use *zêru* to indicate that the party initiating the divorce was at fault. The laws and legal documents which compare cases where the man is at fault with cases where the woman is at fault seem to use explicit statements to identify the guilty party. For example, CH 142, *ANET*, 172, reads "if she was careful and was not at fault, even though her husband had been going out and disparaging her greatly," while CH 143, *ANET*, 172, reads "if she was not careful, but was a gadabout, thus neglecting her house (and) humiliating her husband." The husband's guilt is often indicated by stating that he took a second wife (NB marriage contracts nos. 1, 2, 4, 6, 8, 15-17, 19-20, 25-26, 30, 34; see Roth, *BMA*, 12-15; CE 59, *ANET* 163.) See also Mendelsohn, "On Marriage in Alalakh," 351-357.

44    The phrase עֶרְוַת דָּבָר is a famous crux. The meaning of the phrase was of great significance during the rabbinical period, because it was taken to define the grounds upon which a man could divorce his wife. It was intensely debated. The school of Shimmai understood the phrase to refer to unchastity; the school of Hillel emphasized the word דָּבָר (rather than עֶרְוַת) and took the phrase to refer even to such trivial complaints as the wife having burnt her husband's food. (See also Sir 25:26 and Matt 19:3-9.)

Contemporary scholars are equally divided as to the phrase's meaning. Phillips believes that the Deuteronomic editors added עֶרְוַת דָּבָר to Deut 24:1-4 in order to make sure that the law unambiguously referred to "anything *other than adultery* which the husband found distasteful in his wife," (*AICL*, 112). Neufeld also believes that the Deuteronomic authors may have introduced עֶרְוַת דָּבָר into the Israelite divorce laws; however, in his opinion this represented the first attempt to restrict the man's right to divorce, which had previously been unlimited. Neufeld translates the phrase "some shameful thing" (Ephraim Neufeld, *Ancient Hebrew Marriage Laws* [London: Longmans, Green and Co., 1944], 176).

It is not possible to determine precisely the meaning of the phrase. One can, however, say three things about the clause כִּי־מָצָא בָה עֶרְוַת דָּבָר. First, עֶרְוַת דָּבָר will not refer to adultery; the Deuteronomic authors quite unambiguously ruled that the punishment for adultery was death, not divorce. Second, עֶרְוַת דָּבָר is found in Deut 23:15 (Eng. 23:14), in the command to bury one's excrement outside of the camp, where it seems to refer to anything objectionable. Excrement is not considered unclean (טמא) in the priestly laws. According to the Deuteronomic

Moreover, the phrase with which "hated" is actually contrasted is "if she does not find favor in his eyes because he has found in her some indecency." The first half of the phrase, "if she does not find favor" suggests the woman's subordinate position and the possible arbitrariness of the man's dislike.[45]

The second reason that Westbrook's argument is not persuasive is that he does not adequately take into account the relationship between Deut 24:1-4 and Jer 3:1. Jer 3:1-5 begins with a question: "If a man divorces his wife, and she goes from him and becomes the wife of another man, will he turn to her again? Would not the land be very polluted?" The oracle then goes on to show how much more impossible it would be for Yahweh to take back Judah, who had had not one but many lovers, and who now cried for Yahweh to take her back.

There is a striking similarity between the situation envisioned in the Jeremiah oracle and Deut 24:1-4. A man may not return to a woman whom he had divorced if she has meanwhile married another man. Moreover, there are strong linguistic affinities between the two passages. Both passages use the *piel* of שלח to express divorce. שלח is found with this meaning only in the Deuteronomic laws, Mal 2:16, and Jer 3:1. The language used to describe the woman's remarriage is nearly identical: compare Jer 3:1 וְהָלְכָה מֵאִתּוֹ וְהָיְתָה לְאִישׁ־אַחֵר and Deut 24:2 וְיָצְאָה מִבֵּיתוֹ וְהָלְכָה וְהָיְתָה לְאִישׁ־אַחֵר. The phrase וְהָיְתָה לְאִישׁ־אַחֵר is found only in these two passages. Moreover, the verb שׁוּב is used in both passages. Finally, the motive clauses of both passages state that such action brings guilt upon, or pollutes, the very land (הָאָרֶץ).

Westbrook doubts that Jer 3:1 is related to the Deuteronomic law. His argument is based on the fact that the dissolution of the second marriage is not mentioned in the Jeremiah passage and that the husband is pictured as returning to the woman rather than the woman returning to him. For these reasons Westbrook suggests that the passage refers not to

---

legislation however, it is incompatible with the strict standards of holiness and cleanliness which are to be observed in the camp. Third, while the phrase "found some indecency in her" seems to indicate some objective source of the husband's displeasure, it is clear that the indecency found in the woman was not sufficiently grave to disqualify the woman from marrying a second time.

45   Neufeld, *AHML*, 176; Mayes, *Deuteronomy*, 322; and Phillips, *AICL*, 111-112, have all suggested that "because he found some indecency in her" was added by the Deuteronomic authors to an earlier law. They may well be correct. It is typical of Deuteronomic casuistic laws to include subordinate clauses introduced by כִּי in either the protasis or the apodosis (cf. Deut 15:16). There are no such subordinate clauses introduced by כִּי in the casuistic laws contained in the earlier Book of the Covenant. The use of such subordinate clauses may well be indicative of Deuteronomic editing. If the phrase "found in her some indecency" were secondary, then it is all the more the case that the rationale of the basic law should not be derived from a contrast between it and the verb "hated."

marriage between the former husband and his wife, but to an illicit love affair, and is thus unconnected to the Deuteronomic passage.[46]

Westbrook does not take into account the freedom of the poet/prophet. He expects far too much literalness in what is a poetic interpretation. The development of the metaphor in Jer 3:2-5 stresses Judah's unfaithfulness, and the brazenness and futility of its efforts to return to Yahweh. These are the aspects of the law which the poet cites. Referring to the dissolution of the second marriage would simply clutter the poetry and distract from its message. That the husband in the Jeremiah passage is said to turn to his wife also serves the poem. Judah has tried to return to Yahweh; the issue is not, then, Judah's turning, but Yahweh's. Will Yahweh turn again and take Judah back? The verb שׁוב, used as an auxilary with the meaning "again" in Deut 24:4 is taken up and its meaning turned by Jer 3:1 to create a poignant metaphor. The similarity of the situations depicted by the two passages makes it difficult to believe they are unrelated.[47]

The Jeremiah passage suggests that the law against remarriage was more general than the interpretation proposed by Westbrook. The distinction which Westbrook believes the law makes between divorce with grounds and divorce without grounds is entirely absent from Jer 3:1. Moreover, Jer 3:1-5 places Yahweh in the role of the husband. It is therefore difficult to imagine that the law presupposed by Jeremiah was aimed at curbing the husband's exploitation of his wife.

Finally, Jer 3:1 clearly has to do with purity and pollution. Jer 3:1-5 does not necessarily view the woman in the Deuteronomic law as an adulteress or assume that she was divorced because of sexual misconduct. The Jeremiah passage works as an argument *a minori ad majus*. The lesser pollution is for a husband to take back a wife whom he had divorced if she has meanwhile married another man. The greater pollution is for a husband to take back a wife if she has had many lovers. The contrast is between a legal second marriage (which is nonetheless polluting) and harlotry (how much more polluting!). Jer 3:1 does clearly understand the restored marriage prohibited by Deut 24:4 as a sexual offense, and as polluting.

The third reason that Westbrook's interpretation cannot be sustained is because it is not supported by the motive clauses in Deut 24:4. The first motive clause could be made to fit Westbrook's interpretation by translating it "she has been declared defiled." As argued above, however, the second and third motive clauses indicate that the prohibition is concerned with purity and pollution rather than with rconomic justice.[48]

---

46    Westbrook, "Restoration of Marriage," 405 n. 66.
47    Michael Fishbane, *Biblical Interpretation in Ancient Israel* (Oxford: Clarendon Press, 1985), 307-312, demonstrates the connection between Deut 24:1-4 and Jer 3:1.
48    See pp. 48-51. One may also question whether a widow could have brought wealth

## 6. *Interpreting Deuteronomy 24:1-4 by Analogy to Adultery*

The motive clauses and the interpretation of Deut 24:1-4 found in Jer 3:1 strongly indicate that the law is to be understood in terms of sexual purity and pollution. The prohibited remarriage was viewed as a sexual offense which threatened the very land. It is still not clear why such a restored marriage was seen as polluting.

Partly by a process of elimination, we are pushed to interpret the relationships prohibited by the law as analogous to adultery. Adultery involves a woman having sexual relations with man A, then man B, then

from her second marriage into her third marriage. The question probably has to do with properties derived from the second husband's family. The woman may have been able to take her dowry with her from her first marriage into her second, and from her second into her third. In that case, in relationship to the dowry, the husband would be neither worse nor better off in the restored marriage than he had been in the first marriage. Westbrook considers it likely that the first husband would have been able to keep his wife's dowry. In that case, the woman's share of her family's property would have been lost to her. It seems unlikely that her family would have given their daughter a second dowry after she had been found guilty of indecency.

One must then ask what property belonging to the second husband's family the woman could have brought into her third marriage. Admittedly, it appears to have been customary for the husband to assign to his wife property intended to support her if she were widowed. It seems unlikely, however, that the woman was allowed to take the widow's settlement into a new marriage. It is to be expected that a patrilineal society would try to prevent the alienation of part of the first husband's estate. Efforts to prevent the woman from bringing property from her first husband's family into her second marriage are in fact not uncommon. CH 171b-172, *ANET*, 173, requires that the widow relinquish all claim to her share of her husband's estate if she remarries. CH 177, *ANET*, 174, seeks to ensure that a woman's second husband cannot harm the estate of her first husband's children. One of the marriage contracts at Elephantine, K7, likewise limits the woman's right to the use of her deceased husband's property to the time of her widowhood. If she remarries, the property reverts to his family (Yaron, *Aramaic Papyri*, 74). According to Yaron, such limitations on the widow's use of her deceased husband's property are also found in the Talmud (Mishnah Kethuboth 4.12; Tosefta Kethuboth 11.5, 7; *Aramaic Papyri*, 74 n. 2) and in a Middle Assyrian contract (*Aramaic Papyri*, 74 n. 1). Similarly, while men at Nuzi could appoint their wives guardians over their property and their children, the women were required to relinquish the property in the event that they remarried. See Katarzyna Grosz, "Some Aspects of the Position of Women in Nuzi," in *Women's Earliest Records: From Ancient Egypt and Western Asia*, ed. Barbara S. Lesko (Atlanta: Scholars Press, 1989), 167-180, esp. 177. The one piece of evidence I have found that a widow could take wealth acquired from her deceased husband into a subsequent marriage is NBL 13, *ANET*, 197. NBL 13 allows a widow and her new husband to use the usufruct of her dowry and her widow's settlement throughout her life. It should be noted, however, that the position of women reflected in Neo-Babylonian contracts and laws seems to be considerably higher than the position of women reflected in the biblical materials.

again man A. Deut 24:1-4 prohibits just such a pattern of sexual relations, even when the first and second relationships were legally contracted and legally dissolved.

The restored marriage apparently was seen as making the second marriage adulterous after the fact. Miller interprets the law in this manner: "It is most likely that the potential remarriage was seen as allowing the possibiity for a kind of legal adultery ... The second marriage, while legal, would end up being a violation of the relationship to her first husband when the two were remarried."[49]

In section 2, we noted that Deut 22:13-29 understood adultery as a violation of the husband's rights to exclusive possession of his wife's sexuality. In the Deuteronomic view, adultery violated the communal order precisely because it violated the husband's authority and threatened his need to be certain that his children were his own. Deut 24:1-4 indicates that the Deuteronomic understanding of sexual purity transcends the issue of male authority and perhaps even the issue of paternity. The prohibition against a woman's involvement with first one man, then a second, then again with the first, cannot be explained in terms of claims over her by either man. Indeed, here the threat of pollution and concern for purity actually limit the first husband's prerogatives in relationship to his former wife. Deuteronomy seems to view such intermixed relationships as in and of themselves polluting.

It may not be possible to understand fully why such a pattern of relationships was considered impure. Frymer-Kensky's work on sexuality and pollution suggests a possible way of understanding the matter. Frymer-Kensky, following Mary Douglas, argues that purity beliefs are largely a matter of keeping boundaries intact. The structures of existence must be preserved by keeping different categories firmly separated.[50] Essentially, those things which threaten to break down structures and bring about chaos are polluting.

Frymer-Kensky notes that sex has the power to cross lines between households and thus dissolve categories.[51] Sexual relationships can cross and blur the lines which delineate family from family, clan from clan and even (in the case of bestiality) human from beast. Here, the boundaries of the family and thus the integrity of a man's lineage are threatened by crisscrossing relationships. Sexual relations, whether legal or not, which bind a woman to first one man, then to a second, then again to the first confuse the boundaries which define the (patrilineal) family.

---

49    Miller, *Deuteronomy*, 164.
50    Frymer-Kensky, "Law and Philosophy," and "Pollution, Purification, and Purgation."
      See also Mary Douglas, *Purity and Danger: Analysis of Concepts of Pollution and Taboo* (New York: Praeger, 1966).
51    Frymer-Kensky, "Law and Philosophy," 95.

Here concern for the integrity of the patrilineal family actually leads
to an attempt to limit the authority of a man over a woman. The law
limits the prerogatives of the man in relationship to his former wife. It
does so, however, out of concern for the patrilineal nature of the family.

### 7. The Social and Familial Patterns Assumed by the Law

The primary actor in this law, as in the other Deuteronomic family
laws, is the man. The man takes the wife; the man initiates the divorce;
the man is prohibited from remarrying the wife.

The law is addressed to men. The prohibition is directed against men;
it must, therefore, be the man who could cause the land to incur guilt by
violating the prohibition. The "you" addressed by the final motive clause
seems, therefore, to be in the first place the man and only derivatively, if
at all, the woman.

The law does assume a woman's capacity to act. The wording of v. 2
implies that a woman who had been divorced could contract a second
marriage on her own authority.[52]

The rationale of the law sheds light on the Deuteronomic view of
adultery. That is, it must transcend concern for the husband's authority
over his wife. Deut 24:4 quite precisely denies the first husband's
authority over the woman for the sake of the purity of the community and
in order to support the patrilineal family structure.

---

52   The passage provides some incidental information about divorce. It assumes that the
     man had to give his wife a written bill of divorce. (Reference to a bill of divorce is
     also found in Jer 3:8 and Is 50:1.) The wording of v. 2 apparently assumes that the
     divorced woman will leave the marital home: וְיָצְאָה מִבֵּיתוֹ, "she goes out from his
     house." It must be kept in mind, however, that the first three verses define the facts
     of the specific case addressed by this law; they may not describe general customs of
     divorce. In particular, the fact that the man initiates the divorce in this case does not
     settle the debate over whether women could ever initiate divorce in ancient Israel.

# Chapter Four: The Law of Levirate Marriage and Breach of Modesty: Deuteronomy 25:5-12

Deut 25:5-12 is comprised of two cases. The first, the law of levirate marriage (25:5-10), is primarily concerned with providing an heir for a man who dies without a son. The second, having to do with the seizure of a man's genitals (Deut 25:11-12), penalizes a married woman's breach of modesty. The two laws are joined by catch-words. The law of levirate marriage begins "when brothers (אַחִים) dwell together (יַחְדָּו)"; the breach of modesty law begins "when men fight together (יַחְדָּו), a man and his brother (וְאָחִיו)." The subject of both laws is a wife (אֵשֶׁת) of a man. Both laws have to do with family relationships.

In contrast to the family laws of Deut 21:10-21, which concern relationships of authority, and the laws of Deut 22:13-29, which define and discuss adultery, the two laws in Deut 25:5-12 do not appear to be associated with each other because of specific ideas.[1] We will therefore treat the laws separately. The law of levirate marriage, by far the richer source of information concerning the Deuteronomic view of women's status within the family, will be discussed at some length. The law concerning breach of modesty will then be briefly presented.

## 1. The Law of Levirate Marriage: Deuteronomy 25:5-10

### a. Introduction

The Deuteronomic law of levirate marriage serves multiple purposes.[2] Its principal aim is the provision of male heirs to men who die without

---

[1]   Whether or not one finds thematic ideas which link the two laws depends on how one interprets each of the laws. Phillips interprets 25:11-12 as a case where a woman has physically injured a man's testicles, thereby threatening his ability to have children (*Deuteronomy*, 170). Phillips can then explain the proximity of the two laws; in his view, both concern a man's need for an heir. Calum Carmichael interprets the penalty imposed on the reluctant levir as a symbolic exposure of his genitals. By his interpretation, a law conferring "bold sexual freedom" on a woman in a particular set of circumstances is followed by a law that makes it clear that such sexual freedom is intolerable under any other circumstances (Calum Carmichael, "A Ceremonial Crux: Removing a Man's Sandal as a Female Gesture of Contempt," *JBL* 96 [1977]: 332).

[2]   Levirate relationship may be defined as the practice whereby a male relative of a deceased man is expected to marry or to have sexual relationships with the widow of the deceased man. Different forms of levirate relationships are found in a variety of cultures. This study is not concerned with the function of levirate relationships in other cultures except as they may shed light on the Deuteronomic law. Nor is this study concerned with the origins of the levirate institution in Israel. It will refer to the two narrative accounts of the levirate institution found in the Hebrew Bible (that is, Gen 38 and Ruth, esp. chap. 4) as those accounts contribute to an understanding

sons. This aim includes and ensures the orderly succession of property
from father to son. At the same time, the law secondarily seeks to protect
the widow of the deceased man by providing her with the security and
status of marriage and a son. The first aim obviously presupposes a
patrilineal, patriarchal family structure; the existence and continuation of
the family is defined in terms of its males and, plausibly, in terms of the
land handed down from father to son. The secondary aim is no less
reflective of a male centered asymmetrical family structure. The woman's
primary contribution to the family is the sons whom she bears, while her
economic security is derived from father, husband, or sons. A childless
widow, therefore, is socially anomalous[3] and economically vulnerable.
Levirate marriage protects her by providing her with male support and a
male heir. Moreover, while the law assumes the woman's capacity to act
within the legal sphere, her actions are on behalf of the deceased man.

We will first outline the conditions and rulings set forth in the law of
levirate marriage; second, offer an interpretation of the multi-pronged
purpose of the law; and third, discuss the assumptions concerning women
underlying the law.

### b. *Outline of Deuteronomy 25:5-10*

The Deuteronomic law of levirate marriage consists of two parts. The
first part, v. 5-6, enjoins levirate marriage on the wife and the coparcener
brother of a man who dies without a son. The second part, v. 7-10, deals
with the case where a brother refuses to fulfill the levirate obligation.

The protasis of the first case (v. 5) includes three conditions. First, the
brothers are living together; that is, they have not yet divided their
father's estate.[4]

Second, one of the brothers dies, and third, the deceased brother has
no sons. בֵּן can be translated either inclusively (son or daughter) or
exclusively (son). The meaning of the term in the levirate law, however, is

---

of the Deuteronomic law.

3    Susan Niditch, "The Wronged Woman Righted: An Analysis of Genesis 38," *Harvard
     Theological Review* 72 (1979): 143-149, analyzes the story of Tamar (Gen 38) within
     an anthropological framework which views childless widows as social anomalies.

4    Rofé, "Family and Sex Laws," interprets כִּי־יֵשְׁבוּ אַחִים יַחְדָּו to mean "when brothers
     live on the same estate near each other." He cites Gen 13:6 and 36:7 in support of
     this interpretation. In both of these verses, however, the phrase may well refer to
     joint possession of the land. It is preferable to interpret כִּי־יֵשְׁבוּ אַחִים יַחְדָּו in light
     of the frequent references to brothers who have not yet divided their inheritance
     found in the cuneiform codes, such as MAL B:2, 3, *ANET*, 185, and CE 16, *ANET*,
     262. David Daube, "Consortium in Roman and Hebrew Law," *Juridical Review* 42
     (1950): 71-91, followed by Raymond Westbrook, "The Law of the Biblical Levirate,"
     *RIDA* 24 (1977): 65-87, argues for this reading of the phrase.

to be understood as gender specific. This is shown by the word הַבְּכוֹר,
v. 6; in the Hebrew Bible, הַבְּכוֹר consistently refers to a first-born male.[5]

The apodosis (v. 6) rules that the wife may not marry a stranger, אִישׁ
זָר, that is, a non-family member.[6] Rather, the deceased man's brother is
to marry her.[7] The first male child born of the levirate union is to
"succeed to" (יָקוּם עַל־שֵׁם, literally "stand or rise upon") the "name" of the
deceased.

The sub-case, v. 7-10, sets out the procedure to be followed when the
deceased man's brother is unwilling to provide him an heir. The deceased
man's wife is to bring the matter before the elders, who establish her
brother-in-law's unwillingness to fulfill the levirate obligation.[8] The
woman then performs two symbolic actions before the elders: she pulls a
sandal off the foot of her brother-in-law and she spits at him. The acts are
clearly degrading to the man.[9] Commentators for the most part are

---

5    The LXX and the rabbis interepreted the word inclusively. LXX renders the word
    *spérma*, which is gender-inclusive. The LXX has, however, a distinct bias towards an
    inclusive translation, which is demonstrated by its translation of הַבְּכוֹר. הַבְּכוֹר
    means "first-born," and consistently refers to a male child or animal. The LXX
    renders the term, *padíon*, little child, which is clearly a very free translation. Neufeld,
    *AHML*, 45, and Westbrook, "Biblical Levirate," 65-87, assume the LXX translation
    accommodates the Deuteronomic law to the law of succession which allows
    daughters to inherit (Num 27:8-11). This interpretation is probably correct. The
    rabbinical interpretation results from the clear effort on the part of the rabbis to
    limit the application of the law. This is discussed at some length by Samuel Belkin,
    "Levirate and Agnate Marriage in Rabbinic and Cognate Literature," *Jewish
    Quarterly Review* 60 (1969-1970): 275-329.

6    For זָר used to refer to someone outside of the household, see 1 Kgs 3:18 and Job
    19:15.

7    The nature of the levirate obligation is debated. George Coats, "Widow's Rights: a
    Crux in the Structure of Genesis 38," *CBQ* 34 (1972): 461-466, argues that the widow
    of the deceased had the right to conceive a child by the deceased's brother, but not
    the right to marry the brother. His argument is based largely on the remark that
    Judah did not have further intercourse with Tamar (Gen 38:26). The Tamar/Judah
    story, however, is narrative rather than law; it mentions information important to its
    own story line. Moreover, Tamar's relationship with Judah is an exceptional rather
    than a normal instance of the levirate institution. It cannot serve as evidence for the
    marriage or non-marriage between a brother-in-law and sister-in-law in the typical
    levirate situation. Tamar's observation in Gen 38:14 that she had not yet been given
    to Shelah as a wife is better evidence for the nature of the levirate relationship
    between a sister-in-law and brother-in-law. The language in Deut 25:5-10, וּלְקָחָהּ לוֹ
    לְאִשָּׁה, moreover, is the standard language for marriage. Marriage is explicitly
    mentioned in Ruth.

8    Presumably this releases the woman from obligations to her husband's family.

9    Spitting in someone's face is clearly intended to shame him or her (Is 50:6; Job
    30:10). Num 12:14 alludes to a practice in which a father spits in the face of his
    daughter. The nature and meaning of the practice is unclear. What is clear is that it
    shames the daughter: וְאָבִיהָ יָרֹק יָרַק בְּפָנֶיהָ הֲלֹא תִכָּלֵם שִׁבְעַת יָמִים. The
    withdrawing of the shoe is discussed below.

agreed that the verses mandate public humiliation for the reluctant levir in order to discourage men from seeking to be released from their levirate obligation. Whether or not the acts have additional legal consequences is a matter of debate.[10] Finally, the woman solemnly declares: "Thus it is done to the man who will not build up the house of his brother" (Deut 25:10).[11] The disgraced man's household is henceforth known as "the house of the unsandaled one."

### c. The Aims of Deuteronomy 25:5-10

Unlike the passages previously considered, the wording of Deut 25:5-10 explicitly states the purpose of the law. The purpose of the levirate union is to provide a son, an heir, for the deceased, that his name may not be blotted out of Israel.

The precise meaning of the word שֵׁם (name) within this passage is somewhat elusive. It is unlikely that "succeeding to the name" refers to being given the name of the deceased man in any literal sense. Tamar's sons are not named after Er or Onan; nor is Ruth's son called Mahlon.[12] Israelites did not use surnames, nor did patronymics normally go back more than one or two generations.[13]

Within the context of Deut 25:5-10, שֵׁם seems in the first place to mean "household." Clearly שֵׁם has to do with offspring.[14] It would be nonsensical to say that the first-born male shall succeed to the dead man's "offspring," but he could succeed to and establish the dead man's household. The brother-in-law is accused of refusing to establish the name of his brother (25:7) and refusing to build the household of his brother (25:9); the two phrases seem to carry the same meaning.[15]

Succeeding to the deceased man's name seems to involve inheriting his property. In Ruth 4:5 and 10, the deceased man's name is established

---

10    See below, p. 70-71.

11    As Mayes, *Deuteronomy*, 299, notes, the verbs used to express the woman's declaration, וְעָנְתָה וְאָמְרָה, are a fixed pair found elsewhere in Deuteronomy in the context of formal legal or cultic affirmations (Deut 26:5; 27:14-15).

12    Moreover, Perez, Zerah, and Obed are not listed after Er, Onan, or Mahlon in the genealogies (Num 26:19-20; Ruth 4:21).

13    Etan Levine, "On Intra-familial Institutions of the Bible," *Biblica* 57 (1976): 558.

14    The phrases וְהָקֵם זֶרַע לְאָחִיךְ (Gen 38:8) and לְהָקִים לְאָחִיו שֵׁם (Deut 25:7) seem equivalent. It is clear both from the context of this passage and from the use of the word שֵׁם elsewhere in the Hebrew Bible that offspring (especially but not exclusively male offspring) establish a man's name (1 Sam 24:22; 2 Sam 14:7; 18:18; Is 56:4-5).

      Dean McBride, "The Deuteronomic Name Theology" (Ph.D. diss., Harvard University, 1969), 97-101, has set forth thoroughly convincing evidence that in Egypt, Mesopotamia, and probably in Israel, a man's children were thought to establish his name, and so afford him some sort of ongoing life.

15    V. 10 could then be translated without emendation: "his household in Israel shall be called the house of the unsandaled one."

on his inheritance (לְהָקִים שֵׁם־הַמֵּת עַל־נַחֲלָתוֹ). To be called by someone's name seems to mean to inherit through them in Gen 48:6. Joseph's younger sons are to be called by the names of Ephraim and Manasseh in their inheritance (עַל שֵׁם אֲחֵיהֶם יִקָּרְאוּ בְּנַחֲלָתָם).[16] 2 Sam 14:4ff. and especially Num 27:4 imply that a man's name was somehow established when his own descendants inherited his land.[17]

The term שֵׁם often has to do with the namebearer's personality or essential being. "Establishing the name" may have to do with perpetuating the life or person of the deceased in some way.[18] It would appear that a

16    See also Ez 48:1, where the portions of land assigned to the various tribes are called "names."

17    In the light of this association of name with property, Westbrook has argued that the term שֵׁם has the specific meaning "title" when it is used in the context of the levirate institution ("Biblical Levirate," 70-74). Legally, the levirate institution had a single object: "to prevent the extinction of the deceased's title to his landed inheritance" ("Biblical Levirate," 73). The position taken here is close to that of Westbrook. It differs from Westbrook at three points. First, while Westbrook seems on safe ground when he connects שֵׁם with possessing and passing on the land, his definition of the term as "title" seems overly precise. Westbrook understands the clause "when brothers dwell together" to indicate that the law would not apply when brothers had already divided the property. In that case, the title of the deceased man would have been established during his lifetime and would be perpetuated when his brothers inherited his estate. It is more likely that the perpetuation of the man's name has to do not with the establishment of his title to the land, but with his descendants' continuing possession of his ancestral land. In the story of Zelophehad the rationale for allowing daughters to inherit if their father died without sons implies that the father's name would not be preserved if the land were inherited by the deceased's brothers or other more distant male kin. Yet, according to Westbrook, the man's title to the property would be established by the brother's inheriting the land.
      Second, Westbrook holds that the law of the levirate had only one goal. There seems to be no reason to assume that ancient laws had one and only one aim. I will argue that Deut 25:5-10 was also intended to protect the deceased man's widow. It is even more unlikely that the levirate institution had only one aim; social institutions arise out of complex factors and tend to serve multiple purposes. Westbrook overstates his case.
      Third, Westbrook deliberately limits his exploration of the word שֵׁם in Deut 25:5-10 to an effort to define its univocal legal meaning: "The reasons why the fictional maintenance of a separate title was considered so important are beyond the scope of a legal discussion" ("Biblical Levirate," 79). Within the task Westbrook has set for himself, this limitation is appropriate. This study seeks to examine the world view presupposed by the Deuteronomic family laws as it relates to the role of women, as well as the specific intent of the laws. Therefore, consideration of the significance of the continuation of a man's name need not be excluded from this work.

18    Gen 48:16; 2 Sam 18:18; and Is 56:4-5 are especially suggestive of this. This is not to say, however, that the Deuteronomic law of levirate marriage had to do with providing an heir to carry out rites for the deceased man. Various scholars have suggested that the practice of levirate marriage in Israel (as elsewhere) was associated with ancestor worship; Herbert C. Brichto, "Kin, Cult, Land, and

man's name was established when he left a son to inherit his property and to perpetuate his line, and that this in some way represented the continued existence of the man.[19]

The extreme importance accorded to leaving offspring who would perpetuate one's name is widely attested in the Hebrew Bible. This is especially clear in the threats to blot out a person or nation's name by eradicating their descendants (Is 14:22; Job 18:17-19; see also 1 Sam 24:22). The wise woman of Tekoa is able to persuade David that the principle of leaving a son to establish his father's name is important enough to override the principle that bloodguilt must be avenged (2 Sam 14:4ff.). The law of levirate marriage apparently views the principle of leaving a son to perpetuate the line as more important than the principle of biological paternity[20] or than the prohibitions against sexual relations between a man and his brother's wife.[21]

The wording of Deut 25:5-10 emphasizes the importance of establishing the deceased man's name. Within its five verses the law refers to succeeding to or establishing the name of the deceased, or building his household, five times. The first-born son of the levirate union is to succeed to the name of the deceased brother. The motive given for the law is to prevent the name of the deceased from being blotted out of Israel. In v. 7, the complaint which the woman brings before the elders is that her brother-in-law refuses to establish the name of his brother in Israel. In her declaration to the man (v. 9), the woman refers to him as one who will not build up his brother's household. Finally, the brother-in-law's punishment mirrors his offense. Because he refuses to

---

Afterlife--A Biblical Complex," *Hebrew Union College Annual* 44 (1973): 1-54, in particular has argued that this concept extensively shaped the Deuteronomic law. At least as it relates to Deuteronomic legislation, Brichto's interpretation cannot be seriously entertained. The Deuteronomic authors vehemently opposed the high places where rites for the dead were presumably carried out, and explicitly prohibited such rites (Deut 14:1).

19   This point is argued by Thomas Thompson and Dorothy Thompson, "Some Legal Problems in the Book of Ruth," *VT* 18 (1968): 87-88. Leaving a male heir to inherit one's land is not the only way to establish one's name found in the Hebrew Bible. For example, one's name could also be perpetuated by establishing a memorial stele (2 Sam 18:18; Is 56:4-5).

20   The importance that a man's sons be biologically his own seems to underlie the gravity assigned to the offense of adultery by the Deuteronomic legislation.

21   The relationship of Deut 25:5-10 and Lev 18:16 is debated. Many scholars see a progressive narrowing of the practice of levirate marriage in Israel which culminated in the priestly writers prohibiting it altogether. Others assume Lev 18:16 is applicable only during the lifetime of the husband. Most often the levirate custom is understood as an exception to the laws prohibiting incest. The latter interpretation is preferable; there seems to be no way of establishing a chronological development in the levirate custom based on Gen 38, Ruth, and Deut 25:5-10. The question, however, involves issues which go well beyond the scope of this study.

establish the name of his brother in Israel, the name of his own household is replaced with a degrading name (v. 10).

The law thus is aimed above all at perpetuating the "name" of the deceased, that is, perpetuating his lineage. Westbrook has correctly argued that "the person whose interest the sources regard as being served by the birth of a child is ... the dead husband."[22]

The continuation of the family and the concern for orderly succession of property would also serve the social order. Josephus articulated this aim of the law when he wrote: "This will at once be profitable to the public welfare, houses not dying out ..."[23]

Josephus' explanation continues: "... and property remaining with the relatives."[24] Many modern commentators believe that one of the primary purposes of the law of levirate marriage is to maintain the property of the deceased brother within the family.[25] Those who interpret the levirate law as an attempt to prevent the alienation of property can argue in one of two ways. First, some scholars believe that the widow would inherit her husband's property.[26] According to this view, the widow could take her husband's estate into a future marriage; the offspring of the second marriage might then inherit it. A second possible position is that acquiring the deceased man's land and accepting the responsibility of providing him with an heir were linked; if the deceased man's brother refused to perform the levirate obligation, both land and levirate obligation would go to the next of kin. According to this interpretation, Deut 25:5-10 would be intended to keep the deceased man's property within the immediate family.[27] Neither view is likely.

There are three objections to the view that the widow could inherit the property and bring it into a new marriage. First it is unlikely that a childless widow would normally inherit the property of her husband. The law of succession in Num 27:8-11 does not include the deceased man's widow in its list of possible heirs. There are very few Old Testament references to childless widows apart from Deut 25:5-10; these few provide no evidence that such widows could inherit their husband's property.[28]

---

22  Westbrook, "Biblical Levirate," 70.
23  Josephus, *Antiquities* 4.8.23, cited in Miller, *Deuteronomy*, 165.
24  Ibid.
25  This view is held by Mayes, *Deuteronomy*, 328; Craigie, *Deuteronomy*, 314; Driver, *Deuteronomy*, 282; Clifford, *Deuteronomy*, 282; Driver and Miles, *AL*, 245.
26  This is the position of most commentators.
27  J. J. M. Roberts and Dennis Olson in private communication have taken this position.
28  Women are depicted as owning money or property in Judg 1:14; 17:2-3; 2 Kgs 4:8ff.; 8:1-6; Job 42:15; Ruth 4:3. There are, however, no instances in the Old Testament where a childless widow is depicted as possessing her deceased husband's land. Lev 22:13 refers to a childless widow who returns to her father's household. In Gen 38:11, Judah tells Tamar to go and live as a widow in her father's house; Naomi

Second, Gen 38:9; Ruth 4:6; and Deut 25:7-10 all portray the brother-in-law as reluctant to perform the levirate obligation. According to the Deuteronomic law, it is the sister-in-law who is to bring the matter to the attention of the elders and who humiliates her reluctant brother-in-law. If the woman could inherit a portion of the estate, one would expect the brother-in-law to be the party more interested in the levirate marriage being carried out.

Third, scholars' opinion that the law is intended to prevent the alienation of the deceased man's property from his family usually rests upon a particular interpretation of the woman's removal of the man's sandal. This view accords too much weight to the similarity between Ruth 4:7 and Deut 25:9. According to Ruth 4:7, one drew off one's sandal to validate the redemption or exchange of property. That the woman removes the brother-in-law's sandal in Deut 25:9 is taken either as a symbolic action designed to humiliate the man for having allowed the property to slip away from his family, or as a symbolic act which acually strips the brother-in-law of his rights over the deceased man's share of the property. There are significant differences between the two actions. In Ruth 4:7, the near kinsman removes his own shoe; in Deut 25:9, the woman pulls off her brother-in-law's shoe. Moreover, in Ruth 4:7 all of the parties agree to the transaction; Deut 25:7 depicts the woman as bringing a complaint against her brother-in-law. Westbrook quite correctly notes that the "ceremony in Ruth represents concession of a right, in Deuteronomy it represents failure to perform a duty."[29]

It is quite possible for symbolic actions which are materially similar to have very different meanings.[30] Shoes or the absence of shoes seem to have various symbolic meanings in the Hebrew Bible. Casting a shoe over someone or something is a symbol of power in Psalm 60:10. Going

---

counsels her daughters-in-law to return to their mother's household (Ruth 1:8). Naomi herself is no exception. To be sure, she is depicted as selling a portion of her deceased husband's land (Ruth 4:3). The situation of Naomi, who raised two sons to manhood and then outlived them, is not, however, comparable to the situation of a woman who never bore sons.

What evidence we have from cuneiform legal documents suggests that the surrounding cultures which were most liberal toward women prevented the woman from bringing the property of her first husband into a second marriage. See p. 59 n. 48.

Westbrook dismisses out of hand the possibility that the childless widow could inherit her deceased husband's property: "There is no evidence in the Bible of a widow inheriting land; indeed, all indications are to the contrary" ("Biblical Levirate," 81).

29   Westbrook, "Biblical Levirate," 81.
30   In Babylon, for example, both the act of manumitting a slave and the act of marrying a woman involved pouring oil on the head. Meir Malul, *Studies in Mesopotamian Legal Symbolism*, AOAT 221 (Neukirchen-Vluyn: Neukirchener Verlag, 1988), 40, 161.

barefoot can be a sign of mourning (Ez 24:17, 23) or of humiliation and capture (Is 20:2).

For these reasons, the view that the law seeks to prevent a childless widow from inheriting her husband's property and taking it into a new marriage must be rejected.

The argument which links a kinsman's claim to the deceased man's property to his responsibility to raise up a son for the deceased man is somewhat more plausible; yet it also is not finally convincing. The positive evidence for this view is found in Ruth 4:5, which ties the right of redemption to the levirate obligation.[31] Rowley writes that the redemption of a family member's property and levirate marriage were two separate responsibilities, both of which fell to the גֹּאֵל, the nearest kinsman. In his view, the kinsman was required to acquire Ruth if he purchased Elimelech's field because he could not claim to be גֹּאֵל in one instance without accepting the responsibility of the גֹּאֵל in the other instance.[32] One must ask, however, whether customs governing the right of redemption are the same as those governing inheritance.

More importantly, it is doubtful whether in Deut 25:5-10 the deceased man had held title to property which could be passed on to someone other than his brother. We have interpreted the phrase "when brothers live together" to indicate that the family estate had not yet been divided between the deceased and his brothers when he died. The brothers own the whole of their property together. If that is so, the deceased man had held no land to which he had absolute title. According to Daube, the surviving brother "was owner of all the property even while his brother was alive, and now, on the latter's death, he just goes on being owner."[33]

---

31    The text of Ruth 4:5 is problematic. The MT reads: וַיֹּאמֶר בֹּעַז בְּיוֹם־קְנוֹתְךָ הַשָּׂדֶה
מִיַּד נָעֳמִי וּמֵאֵת רוּת הַמּוֹאֲבִיָּה אֵשֶׁת־הַמֵּת קָנִיתִי לְהָקִים שֵׁם־הַמֵּת עַל־נַחֲלָתוֹ. The word קניתי is vocalized (*Qere*) to be read קָנִיתָ. Derek R. G. Beattie, "The Book of Ruth as Evidence for Israelite Legal Practice," *VT* 24 (1974): 251-267, has presented the strongest argument for maintaining the *Kethibh* (קָנִיתִי). In his opinion, Boaz asserts that he will acquire Ruth for himself the day the nearer kinsman redeems the field. Beattie's interpretation does not fit within the larger context of the story, however. If Boaz could have married Ruth without the other man's relinquishing his claims, there would be no reason for the encounter at the gate, nor would Boaz's reference to the nearer kinsman in Ruth 3:12-13 make any sense. Most commentators therefore accept the *Qere*, and interpret the verse as linking redemption of the property to perfomance of the levirate obligation. For further discussion of the textual problems, see Edward F. Campbell, *Ruth*, Anchor Bible (Garden City, N.Y.: Doubleday, 1975), 146-147.

32    Harold H. Rowley, "The Marriage of Ruth," in *The Servant of the Lord and Other Essays on the Old Testament* (Oxford: Basil Blackwell, 1952), 171-194.

33    Daube, "Consortium," 76. MAL A:25-26, *ANET*, 182, provides some confirming evidence that the disposal of a man's share of his father's property when the estate had not been divided was quite different from when it had been divided. According to Driver and Miles, *AL*, 193-196, MAL A:25 mandates that if brothers have not

Ancient Israel's concern that ancestral lands remain within the family underlies several of its institutions. The institution of redemption of property and that of the jubilee year, for example, were intended to prevent the final alienation of property. It is unlikely, however, that such a concern lies behind the institution of levirate marriage in general, or the Deuteronomic law of the levirate in particular.[34]

Josephus' discussion of the law of levirate marriage goes on to explain that it was intended to protect widows: "And it will moreover bring the women an alleviation of their misfortune to live with the nearest kinsman of their former husbands."[35] Neufeld argues that the primary aim of levirate marriage was to protect the childless widow who, he believes, had no other means of support.[36] He believes that the drafters of the law refrained from explicitly stating its primary objective (securing the welfare of widows) because they knew that social, economic, and religious motives would have a greater appeal to the people than such a moral concern.[37]

Neufeld too easily dismisses the explicit and repeated explanation of its aims found in the law of levirate. His explanation is *ad hoc*. Elsewhere, Deuteronomic legislation is replete with moral exhortation. Providing for the widow's welfare may well be a secondary aim of the law, however. It seems clear that the institution of levirate marriage would have provided the wife of the deceased man an important means of economic security and social status.[38]

The second part of the law, v. 7-10, is a concession to the brother-in-law, in that it allows him to reject his levirate obligation. It also releases the woman from her obligations. The Tamar story (Genesis 38) shows that a woman's obligations to her husband's family were not terminated by his death. Tamar is under the authority of her father-in-law; her sexuality is his to dispose. When Judah is told that

---

divided their inheritance and one of them dies, the surviving brothers may claim any ornaments which the deceased man had given to his wife. MAL A:26, on the other hand, concerns the case where the brothers had already divided the paternal estate. In that case, ornaments which a husband had given his wife became the property of the man's sons upon his death. If there were no sons, the wife of the deceased man might inherit the ornaments.

34    The law of levirate marriage does relate to the Deuteronomic concern for social order in that it supports the continuity of the family and orderly succession from father to son.

35    Josephus, *Antiquities* 4.8.23, cited in Miller, *Deuteronomy*, 165.

36    Neufeld, *AHML*, 29. He notes that the widow would also contribute her labor and administration skills to the levir's household.

37    Ibid, 33.

38    Eryl Davies, "Inheritance Rights and the Hebrew Levirate Marriage," parts 1, 2, *VT* 31 (1981): 138-144, 257-268, has suggested that mothering a son who was heir to the deceased man's property would allow the woman to continue to manage her dead husband's estate.

Tamar has become pregnant, he sentences her to death. The Deuteronomic law required a brother-in-law who was unwilling to undertake the levirate marriage to say so publicly. The widow would then be released from her obligation to him.

The overriding concern of Deut 25:5-10 is the perpetuation of a "name" for the deceased man. Above all else, the law served the interest of the deceased man, and the continuity of the patriarchal family. It also likely aimed at protecting the widow and ensuring the orderliness of the succession of property.

### d. *Social and Familial Patterns Assumed by Deuteronomy 25:5-10*

Deut 25:5-10 clearly presupposes a patrilineal, patriarchal family structure. Its overarching concern is the perpetuation of the man's name, that is, the continuation of the man's lineage and, presumably, the continued ownership of the man's property by his male descendants. The use of the term שׁם elsewhere in the Hebrew Bible (and Mesopotamian documents) to express the essence of one's personhood may suggest that the law has to do in some sense with the deceased man's continued existence. At least it has to do with a basic sense of the ongoing meaning of the man's life.[39] The law depicts the widow as sharing this perspective; her complaint is not that the brother-in-law has failed to provide her with a son, but that he has failed to build the household of her deceased husband.[40]

The central importance of property-progeny-name as carried down from father to son suggests that the importance of the role played by women was correspondingly derivative or secondary. Women did not carry on the family name; they did not regularly inherit family property (Deut 21:15-17). In a patrilineally structured society, women participate in the lineage of their husbands; they do not have lineages of their own. Deut 25:5-10 thus raises some questions about the continued existence of the lives of women, or the ongoing meaning of their lives. Presumably such meaning was understood to be derived from women's contribution to the continuation of their husbands' lineage when they mothered sons.

The secondary aim of Deut 25:5-10, the protection of widows, also presupposes a patriarchal family structure. The woman's economic security was derived primarily through her husband or through mothering

---

39  Katharine Doob Sakenfeld, "In the Wilderness, Awaiting the Land: The Daughters of Zelophehad and Feminist Interpretation," *Princeton Seminary Bulletin* 9 (1988): 181-186, offers three interpretations of Num 27. According to one interpretation, the central issue of the narrative is the existential concern of male Israelites that their name be perpetuated through their sons. Sakenfeld describes this concern as having to do with the basic meaning of life and death.

40  Sakenfeld, "In the Wilderness," 183, points out that Zelophehad's daughters quite plausibly also "participated in this (patriarchal) cultural assumption."

a male heir for her husband. Her social status was linked to her role in the family. Susan Niditch has pointed out that there were two socially affirmed roles for women in Israelite society: a woman could be a virgin in her father's house or a childbearing wife. The childless widow was a social anomaly.[41] The levirate law protected the widow economically and resolved her anomalous social status. It provided a protection that would be necessary and comprehensible only in a patriarchal society.

The law presupposes an asymmetrical structure of authority within the family. A man had a duty to marry the wife of his deceased, son-less brother; he could, however, refuse to do so. The law gives no indication that the wife of the deceased man had any choice. The woman's obligations to her deceased husband's family were not terminated by his death.

Deut 25:5-10 presupposes that the woman is able to act within the legal sphere. The woman brings her complaint against the reluctant brother-in-law before the elders; she is the plaintiff in the case.[42] Moreover, it is the woman who carries out the punishment against the man who has refused to marry her and father a son for her dead husband. She is in some way the avenger of the deceased.

She appears to act before the elders in a representative capacity. Her complaint and her solemn declaration to the brother-in-law are couched in terms of the interests of her dead husband, not in terms of her own interests. Or, rather, her interests appear to coincide with and be subsumed under the interests of the deceased.

### 2. Breach of Modesty: Deuteronomy 25:11-12

The following law, Deut 25:11-12, treats a case where a married woman intervenes in a fight between her husband and another man by seizing the genitals of her husband's opponent. The penalty laid down for the woman is that her hand is to be amputated.

The law has some peculiar characteristics. First, in contrast to the other stipulations we have studied (such as the adultery laws or the law of levirate marriage) it concerns a set of circumstances that cannot have occured very often. Second, apart from the laws of talion (Ex 21:23-25; Lev 24:17-22; Deut 19:21) it is the only biblical law to prescribe physical

---

41  Niditch, "The Wronged Woman Righted," 144-146.
42  To the best of my knowledge, this is the only case in the Hebrew Bible where a woman by herself (without a man) brings a complaint before the elders. There are several instances where women appeal to other male authorities for justice (Num 27; 2 Sam 14:4ff.; 1 Kgs 3:16-27; 2 Kgs 8:1-6). The narrative of 2 Kgs 8:1-6 does not say whether the woman's husband was still living. In each of the other passages cited, the woman appealing directly to judicial authority is either a widow, a harlot, or an orphan; she therefore has no male to represent her.

mutilation as a penalty.[43] These peculiarities suggest that the law is intended to lift up some particular point rather than to provide guidance for the treatment of a typical case.[44] The penalty suggests the severity of the offense in the eyes of the redactors of the law.

This study accepts the frequently proposed interpretation that the particular point raised by the law has to do with the seriousness of a woman's breach of modesty.[45] A woman's loyalty to her husband was surely considered a positive value; the desire to come to his defense would have been an admirable motive. That the woman is punished for seizing a man's genitals even if she has acted in order to rescue her husband shows that for a married woman to have sexual contact with a man other than her husband is abhorrent, even under extenuating circumstances. This in turn emphasizes the gravity of the offense. The penalty also underscores that gravity. Severing the woman's hand is an example of "mirror punishment"; the penalty affects the peccant member.[46] It is also an unusually severe punishment, manifesting the abhorrence with which the redactors viewed breach of modesty on the part of the woman. The use of the euphemism מְבֻשָׁיו, "that which excites shame,"[47] for "his genitals" also indicates that the concern of the law is the woman's lack of modesty or shamelessness.[48]

---

43   The severance of the part of the body especially implicated in an offense is not uncommon in the cuneiform codes. The CH, for example, rules that the offender's hand shall be cut off in the case of a son who strikes his father (195, *ANET*, 175); of a surgeon whose surgery results in the patient's death or loss of an eye (218, *ANET* 175); and of a brander who cuts off the slave mark of someone else's slave (226, *ANET*, 176). If a wet nurse whose charge has died under her care accepts another baby to nurse without informing the parents about the earlier death, her breast is to be cut off (194, *ANET*, 175). An adopted son who rejects his foster parents is to lose his eye for looking away from them (192, *ANET*, 175). Such "mirror punishments" are also common in the MAL; the lip of a man who kisses another man's wife is to be cut off (A:9, *ANET*, 181); as will be discussed below, if a woman grabs a man's genitals and injures a testicle, her finger is to be amputated.

44   von Rad, *Deuteronomy*, 155, writes: "People have certainly been justified in inquiring why the decision based on such a peculiar case had to be raised to a law of general validity."

45   Driver, *Deuteronomy*, 285, writes: "Immodesty, even when extenuating circumstances are present, is to be checked as stringently as possible." This view is also held by Weinfeld, *DDS*, 292; Shalom M. Paul, "Biblical Analogues to Middle Assyrian Laws," *Religion and Law: Biblical-Judaic and Islamic Perspectives*, ed. E. B. Firmage et al. (Winona Lake, Ind.: Eisenbrauns, 1990), 338; Dale Patrick, *Old Testament Law* (Atlanta: John Knox Press, 1985), 138; Miriam Shrager, "A Unique Biblical Law," *Dor le Dor* 15 (1986-1987): 190-194; David Daube, "The Culture of Deuteronomy," *ORITA* 3 (1969): 36-37.

46   See n. 43 above.

47   BDB, 102. The word is a *hapax legomena*.

48   Another plausible explanation of the rationale of the law is offered by Driver and Miles, *AL*, 30-31; Cardascia, *Lois Assyriennes*, 108-109; and Smith, *Deuteronomy*,

Phillips offers an alternative rationale for the law. He believes that the penalty is more severe than breach of modesty would warrant and argues that the law assumes that the woman has physically injured the victim. The severity of the penalty would be accounted for by the fact that the injury threatens the man's ability to have children.[49] The law would then show how *lex talionis* could be extended when it was not possible to apply it literally.

This interpretation, though attractive, is not finally convincing. The main evidence for such an interpretation is the parallel law found in the Middle Assyrian code, MAL A:8.[50] The Assyrian law concerns a woman who seizes and damages a man's genitals in the midst of a brawl. If one testicle is damaged, she is to lose one finger; if both are damaged or become inflamed, both of the woman's [eyes? breasts?] are to be gouged out.[51]

As has often been remarked, the similarities between Deut 22:11-12 and MAL A:8 are striking. Both cases concern a brawl in which a woman seizes a man's genitals; in both cases the woman is punished by the severance of a hand or part of a hand. The difference between the laws is also striking, however. MAL A:8 specifies quite precisely the degree of physical injury that the woman inflicts on the man, and correlates the penalty to the degree of injury. Deut 25:11-12 does not mention physical injury at all.

Arguments from silence are admittedly dangerous. The drafters of the ancient Near Eastern laws assumed a body of knowledge on the part of their audience.[52] For example, the absence of a clause granting the father of a violated girl the right to withhold his daughter from marriage to the man who violated her in Deut 22:28-29 does not necessarily mean that Deuteronomic law precluded him from doing so. That right may have been assumed.[53] Knowledge of the degree of injury is not something that the redactors of 25:11-12 could assume, however. Unless it were specified, the injury could range from serious damage to negligible damage. Correlation between the degree of injury and the penalty inflicted is at the heart of the Assyrian law. The penalty in Deut 25:11-12

---

289. They suggest that it reflects respect or reverence for the man's genitals as the organ of regeneration. The euphemism מְבֻשָׁיו, however, suggests that the underlying rationale has to do with the shamefulness of the woman's act.

49    Phillips, *AICL*, 94; Phillips is followed by Craigie, *Deuteronomy*, 316.

50    *ANET*, 181.

51    The text is broken at the point which would specify which of the woman's organs is to be gouged out. For a discussion of possible ways of reconstructing of the text, see Paul, "Analogues," 337.

52    For further discussion of the problems of arguing from silence see Westbrook, *SBCL*, 1-8.

53    It may also represent an extension of state control.

appears to be the same regardless of whether the woman has or has not physically injured the man.

Other arguments adduced for interpreting the case as punishing the woman for physically injuring the man are less weighty. Phillips writes that the *hiphil* stem of חזק denotes a violent act.[54] The verb can be used of violence, including sexual assault.[55] It can also, however, refer to holding in the sense of sustaining, supporting, cleaving to, or guiding.[56] Phillips' argument that the penalty in Deut 25:11-12 is too severe for a breach of modesty imposes twentieth century values on an ancient text.[57] The common reading of this rather odd law, that it penalizes breach of modesty on the part of women, is still the more persuasive interpretation of the text.

---

54   Phillips, *AICL*, 95.
55   Deut 22:25; 2 Sam 13:11.
56   Paul, "Analogues," 335 n. 6, states that the *hiphil* stem of חזק refers to "some sort of violent seizing or grasping" when it is used in conjunction with the preposition בְּ. This is contradicted, however, by the use of the *hiphil* of חזק and בְּ to refer to God's benevolent guidance in Jer 31:32 and Is 45:1.
57   That we may not assume a correspondence between modern assessments of the gravity of an offense and ancient assessments of the offense is shown by the penalties assigned by Deuteronomy to the rape of an unbetrothed virgin (Deut 22:28-29), and to a girl who enters into a marriage without her virginity intact (Deut 22:20-21). Deuteronomy imposes the death penalty on the latter, financial compensation and compulsory reparative marriage on the former. Twentieth century American laws treat the former as a serious felony, while the latter would not be considered a crime at all.

# PART TWO: Analysis of the View of Women Found Within the Deuteronomic Family Laws

## Chapter Five: The Laws as Cultural Artifact

### 1. *Introduction*

The Deuteronomic redactors presumably included the particular family laws now found within the Deuteronomic corpus for specific reasons: to protect certain rights or uphold certain values. The exegetical study in chapters 1-4 examined the rhetoric and logic of these laws and their cuneiform and biblical background in order to explicate their specific legal intent. The study's concluding chapter will analyze the overall purpose served by the inclusion of these family laws in the Deuteronomic corpus as that purpose relates to women.

The laws, however, provide us with information apart from the specific purpose of the lawmakers or redactors. That is, the laws presuppose certain social institutions. They are a kind of "cultural artifact" which points to familial or social patterns that the lawmakers and redactors took for granted. Laws make sense in certain social contexts, but not in others. Moreover, the specific conditions and judgments of the laws often implicitly or explicitly provide information which is incidental to the main thrust of the laws. Such incidental information is as important to understanding the Deuteronomic view of women as is articulating the purpose or thrust of the laws. This chapter will seek to identify the family patterns and the status of women within the family that are presupposed by the Deuteronomic family laws.

In particular, it will seek to identify ways in which the laws presuppose gender symmetry or asymmetry. In this connection, Carol Meyers has recently criticized the frequently over-facile use of the term "patriarchy." She notes that the term has been used in ways that obscure the differences between varying cultures. As Meyers writes, "male dominance does not have a universal content or shape."[1] Meyers also argues that women's status in a given society has discrete aspects. No one of these aspects can be used to determine the overall status of women within a particular society. Finally, Meyers cautions against evaluating gender differences in light of twentieth century experience or values.[2]

Meyers' criticism of an undifferentiated use of the concept "patriarchy" is well taken. Even within the ancient Near East, one may not

---

1   Carol Meyers, *Discovering Eve: Ancient Israelite Women in Context* (New York: Oxford University Press, 1988), 30.

2   Ibid., 29-40.

speak of patriarchy in this manner. Each of the cultures surrounding Israel is characterized by the dominance of men over women in at least some aspects of life. Yet the position of women in those cultures, at least as it is suggested by the law codes, varies widely. Nor, as Meyers asserts, is "women's status" a homogeneous concept. A culture may restrict some aspects of the lives of women more or less than it restricts other aspects. Finally, asserting the subordinate status of women within a particular family pattern does not mean that the women are not seen as active, contributing members of their families or that they have no legal rights.

Nonetheless, one may examine specific ways in which the Deuteronomic texts presuppose the subordination of women to men. In light of the claims that have been put forth by Rémy, Weinfeld, Phillips, and Steinberg concerning the supposedly more humane or more egalitarian view of women held by the Deuteronomic redactors, it is important to examine evidence that points to the gender asymmetry presupposed by the laws as well as to the gender symmetry they presume.[3] This chapter will examine ways in which the Deuteronomic family laws presuppose the subordination of women to men, as well as ways in which the laws presuppose that male authority is limited or that women are active agents.

Three caveats are in order. First, the family patterns implied by the laws reflect the views of the Deuteronomic redactors; they may or may not reflect actual cultural and legal practices. Archaelogical finds from cultures surrounding Israel have allowed for some comparison between ideals expressed in the laws and actual practices expressed in contracts and trial records. Discrepancies between law and practice have been documented.[4]

Second, it is possible that the language of the law may represent legal convention. For example, the drafters of the laws may have used gender

---

3    See pp. 5-6. The picture of the status of women which emerges from the Deuteronomic laws is basically congruent with the picture of women in the OT in general as it has been sketched by Pedersen, *Israel*, vol. 1, 46-81; de Vaux, *Ancient Israel*, 19-40; and Bird, "Images of Women," 48-57.

4    See Samuel Greengus, "Law in the OT," *IDBSup*, 532-537. This discrepancy is illustrated by the difference between the picture of women's status which emerges from reading the MAL, and the picture which emerges from certain Middle Assyrian marriage contracts. The MAL suggest that Assyrian women were subject to severe restrictions. According to MAL A:59, *ANET*, 185, a husband could punish and humiliate his wife apparently at will. There is no hint in the laws that a woman could obtain a divorce at her initiative (Driver and Miles, *AL*, 268-271). Two documents appear to give the wife a right of divorce equal to that of the husband, according to E. Lipinski, "The Wife's Right to Divorce in the Light of an Ancient Near Eastern Tradition," *JLA* 4 (1981): 19 and n. 40.

Any particular woman's actual rights and obligations within marriage had a great deal to do with the power and prestige of her family, and the ability of her relatives to negotiate positive marital conditions for her.

specific terms in a generic way. Neo-Babylonian laws concerning marriage arrangements, for instance, consistently refer to the bride's agent as her "father."[5] Yet the bride's father serves as her agent in only thirteen out of the thirty-nine Neo- and Late Babylonian marriage contracts where the agent is known.[6] The word "father" in the Neo-Babylonian law indicates the bride's typical agent; the wording of the laws was not intended to rule that only the father could serve in this capacity. Similarly, Deut 22:19 and 22:29 assume that the father acts as the agent of his daughter's marriage. The stories of Hagar, Rebekah, and Samson, however, suggest that mothers and brothers could be involved in arranging marriages.[7]

Third, the Deuteronomic family laws reflect the particular concerns of the Deuteronomic redactors. The redactors' selection of laws itself attests to their view of and evaluation of the status of women. The selectivity of the laws, however, inevitably limits what can be inferred. The laws are silent about such subjects as the wife's dowry, divorce or widowhood settlement. In view of the laws' selectivity, their silence on such topics cannot be interpreted as evidence that the Deuteronomists rejected such practices. Like the other ancient Near Eastern law codes, the Deuteronomic laws take for granted a large body of customary law. There are simply large gaps in what may be inferred from the Deuteronomic code.

## 2. Woman's Status Defined by her Role in a Male Headed Family

The Deuteronomic family legislation is not interested in "women" per se. Rather, the laws refer to women in terms of their roles of mother, daughter, and wife. In each of these roles, the woman's status is defined in relationship to the family, and especially in relationship to the male

---

5    NBL 8-10, *ANET*, 197. See also Roth, *BMA*, 30-31.
6    Martha Roth, "Age at Marriage and the Household: A Study of Neo-Babylonian and Neo-Assyrian Forms," *Comparative Studies in Society and History* 29 (1987): 715-747, esp. 724, table 1. Other agents are: the bride's father and mother acting together (1); the bride's mother (8); the bride's mother and brother acting together (3); the bride herself (3); and the bride's brother (12). The discrepancy between what one would deduce from the language of the laws and the actual practice reflected in the marriage agreements is probably greater in late Babylonian legal documents than it would be in the Deuteronomic period. There is much more evidence that late Babylonian women were able to hold property and transact business arrangements than there is evidence that ancient Israelite women were able to do so. It is correspondingly less likely that the mother of a bride or the bride herself would act as her agent, especially in a first marriage. Nonetheless, the Neo-Babylonian documents caution us to interpret the language of marriage laws as typical rather than restrictive.
7    Gen 21:21; 24:50-60; Judg 14:2-3.

head of the family. We will briefly discuss the dependence of the woman
on a male-headed family in the view of the Deuteronomic legislation, and
then will examine the view of mother, daughter, and wife found in the
Deuteronomic family laws.

There can be no doubt that, in the Deuteronomic view, a woman's
economic security and social worth depended upon her relationship to
her father, husband, or sons. The laws which seek to protect vulnerable
women presuppose that they are vulnerable precisely because they are
either husbandless or threatened with being husbandless. The secondary
aim of the law of levirate marriage, we have argued, is to provide
economic security and a socially acceptable status for the deceased man's
wife. Such a law was necessary precisely because a wife was dependent
upon her husband, or a male heir of her husband.

Similarly, Deut 22:28-29 requires a man who rapes an unbetrothed
virgin to marry her and never divorce her. The ruling makes sense in a
society where a raped girl is either ineligible for marriage or eligible for
only a very poor marriage, and where she is dependent upon marriage for
her economic well-being.[8] Deut 22:19, which prohibits a man who has
spurned and slandered his bride from ever divorcing her similarly
presupposes a social context in which the bride's social and economic
welfare can be secured only through marriage, and in which it would be
difficult for the maligned woman to find another husband.[9] The
injunctions to assist, include, or treat justly the אַלְמָנָה[10] also presuppose
the precariousness of the existence of a woman who is deprived of a
man's support.[11]

Deuteronomic law defines a woman's legal status (as well as her social
and economic position) in terms of her relationships to men. Whether or
not she is married determines what behaviors of or towards a woman are
considered capital offenses. "Marriage is the primary determinant of [her]
legal status and obligation."[12]

---

8    See p. 103, n. 24.
9    Both Deut 22:13-19 and 22:28-29 also protect the girl's father, in that he is relieved
     of the responsibility of maintaining an unmarriageable daughter, and in that the
     honor of his family is secured.
10   Deut 14:29; 16:11, 14; 24:17, 22; 26:12.
11   Paula Hiebert, "'Whence Shall Help Come to Me?' The Biblical Widow," in *Gender
     and Difference in Ancient Israel*, 125-141, argues that the biblical אַלְמָנָה is not any
     widow, but one who is without a male to support her. In contrast to Hiebert, we
     interpret אַלְמָנָה as any woman whose husband is dead. See Gen 38:11 and 2 Sam
     14:4ff.
12   Bird, "To Play the Harlot," 77. Bird notes that it is only for women, not for men, that
     marriage is the primary determinant of legal status, a distinction that is part of a
     "general pattern of asymmetry in gender-related roles, values and obligations" ("To
     Play the Harlot," 79).

There can also be no doubt that the Deuteronomic legislation defines the family in terms of its males. The family here, as elsewhere in the Old Testament, is referred to as the בֵּית אָב, "father's household" (Deut 22:21).[13] The life of the family is perpetuated through its sons and (presumably) through the land carried down from father to son.[14] The patrilineal structure of the family is best seen in the law of the levirate, with its stress on each man's need for a son to inherit his land and perpetuate his name.[15] The law of primogeniture (Deut 21:15-17) also presupposes a patrilineal family. The case concerns a polygynous situation; polygyny presupposes that the family is defined in terms of its male head. Morever, the law of primogeniture assumes that the father's property normally will be inherited by his sons.

The Deuteronomic family is patrilocal; the man brings his wife into his household (21:12) or into the household which he shares with his brothers (25:5). If her husband divorces her, a woman leaves her husband's household (Deut 21:14; 24:2-3).

Meyers does not question the fact that the status of the woman was determined by her role within the family. Nor does she challenge the patrilineal nature of the Israelite family. Rather, Meyers questions whether the status of women within the patrilineal family was necessarily subordinate. Meyers' criticisms press those of us who assert that the biblical texts reflect the subordinate role of women to define those relationships more precisely.[16] The remainder of this chapter examines the status of women as mothers, as daughters, and as wives, assumed by the Deuteronomic family legislation.

a. *Mother: Gender Symmetry and Asymmetry in the Status of Parents*

It is commonly asserted that an Israelite woman attained her highest status in society when she became a mother. Certainly this is true of the Deuteronomic perspective. In some aspects of their parental roles, men and women are treated with a remarkable degree of parity. Other passages presuppose asymmetrical roles for the mother and the father.

The Deuteronomic laws assume that children are obligated to carry out mourning rituals for their mothers as well as their fathers. The law of the captive bride mandates that the captive woman is to mourn her parents for one month before her master/husband can take her as his

---

13  See also Deut 21:12; 24:5; 25:9, 10.

14  The patrilineal, patrilocal structure of the ancient Israelite family is no longer subject to much debate. As Meyers notes, "There can be no doubt about the existence of a system of lineage reckoned through male ancestry and regulating the transmission of property through the male line in ancient Israel" (*Discovering Eve*, 39).

15  Deut 25:5-10 and see p. 73.

16  Meyers, *Discovering Eve*, 24-46.

wife (Deut 21:13). It is unlikely that a foreign captive would be required to mourn both mother and father unless native Israelites also mourned their mothers and fathers alike.

The Deuteronomic family law that provides the clearest evidence of ways in which the mother's status was regarded as equal to the father's is that of the rebellious son, Deut 21:18-21. Echoing the fifth commandment, this law resolutely asserts the authority of the mother and the father over their wayward son.[17] It holds the mother and the father responsible for the conduct of their son,[18] and plausibly grants the mother as well as the father authority over their son in relationship to the rest of the community.[19] In this law, the roles of the mother and the father are the same.

The syntax of Deut 21:18-21 also treats the father and the mother with a striking parity. Both the mother and father seize the son and take him before the elders. Even in court, the mother and father act and testify together. The son is referred to as "our son." The charge is that he has refused to listen to the voice of his father and the voice of his mother.

In contrast, the syntax of the law of the slandered bride (Deut 22:13-19) does not treat the mother and father with such parity. The father and mother go to court over a matter concerning their child in this law, also. The passage, however, presumes the priority of the father; the

---

17　The law is in complete continuity with predeuteronomic biblical traditions which assert the authority of the mother as well as the father. Biblical commandments and laws requiring one to respect both parents are found at Ex 20:12; 21:15, 17; Lev 20:9; Deut 5:16; 27:20. Wisdom literature also asserts the authority and responsibility of the mother as well as the father. Sons are commanded to obey or respect their mothers as well as their fathers in Prov 1:8; 6:20; 23:22. The behavior of the son is said to gladden or to disgrace the mother as well as the father in Prov 10:1; 15:20; 19:26; 23:24-25; 29:15; 30:17. Other proverbs warn against maltreating the mother and the father: 20:20; 28:24; 30:17.

18　Unlike other biblical commands and laws demanding respect towards parents, Deut 21:18-21 cites anti-social behavior not directly aimed at the parents as a manifestation of disrespect for them. That the son's drunkenness and gluttony is taken as rebelliousness against his father and mother implies the parents' responsibility for their son's public behavior.

19　It is possible that the parents were required to bring their incorrigible son before the elders because they had to surrender their authority over him before he could be put to death. Two other biblical passages suggest that the parents' consent was required before punishment could be inflicted upon their son. In 2 Sam 14:7, the wise woman of Tekoa tells David that the clan has demanded that she surrender her son to them so that they might avenge his murder of his brother. Apparently the clan could not just seize and execute the culprit in this hypothetical case. Similarly, Judg 6:30 depicts the men of his town demanding that Joash surrender his son Gideon to them so that they could execute him. These two passages are both predeuteronomic and thus reflect earlier conditions; however, it is plausible that the authority of the parents over their own children continued to be strong enough to make their consent necessary for their son's execution.

mother plays a subordinate role. The father and the mother both present evidence before the elders, but only the father speaks. Moreover, in contrast to the language of 21:20, where the parents refer to "our son," in 22:16, the father calls the girl "my daughter." One must ask why.

It seems likely that the difference in the ways the laws treat the mother has to do with the difference between intra-family and inter-family disputes. Deut 21:18-21 has to do with intra-family matters: the parents' relationship to their own offspring. Within the family, dependent minors owed obedience to their mother just as they did their father.[20] By contrast, Deut 22:13-19 has to do with an inter-family dispute. The father of the girl, and her mother, are charging the head of another household with slandering their family's honor in the process of trying to defraud them of the bridewealth. The father's testimony also refers to an inter-family matter. He gave his daughter to a man, the head of a different household. The laws suggest that the father had primary authority in matters related to his dependent minors that involved other families: the family's honor, the family's economy, and its alliance with other families through marriage.

### b. Daughter: Gender Symmetry and Asymmetry in the Status of Minors

The Deuteronomic family laws (and other Deuteronomic texts) presuppose that the status of the daughter both resembles the status of the son and differs from it. The status of the daughter and that of the son resemble each other in three ways.

First, both owe obedience to their parents; the penalty for flouting parental or paternal authority is death for either the son or the daughter. The son's obligation, set forth in Deut 21:18-21, has already been discussed. Deut 22:20-21 is in some ways parallel to Deut 21:18-21. It has aptly been called the "law of the rebellious daughter." The motive clause of the law (Deut 22:21) explains that the unchaste bride must be put to death because she has played the harlot while in the household of her father; that is, while under her father's authority. The similarities between the penalty, wording, and motive clauses of the two laws suggest that they may have been intended to be read as parallel cases dealing with rebellious offspring.[21]

Second, the laws suggest that daughters as well as sons are obliged to perform mourning rituals for their parents (Deut 21:13).

Third, Deuteronomic texts apart from the family laws show that daughters as well as sons were valued by their parents. This is perhaps

---

20    This parity would have been limited by the fact that the wife was subject to her husband in significant ways.

21    Both concern unruly offspring, the penalty for both is that "all the men of his or her city" shall stone the culprit. Both conclude with the expurgation formula: "And you shall purge the evil from your midst."

most apparent in the curses with which the community was threatened if they failed to keep the Deuteronomic laws. These curses include the exile or loss of sons and daughters (Deut 28:32, 41); and the threat that famine would be so great that one would eat one's sons and daughters, or would withhold food from them (Deut 28:53, 56). Such threats make sense only if daughters were indeed valued. Daughters are also included along with sons in the commands to rejoice before Yahweh with all of one's family (Deut 12:12, 18; 16:11, 14).[22]

Nonetheless, there are significant differences in the status of the daughter and the son presupposed by the Deuteronomic family laws. These are seen in part in the nature of the charges brought against the rebellious son and the rebellious daughter. The son is guilty of irresponsible public behavior: drinking, gluttony. This is behavior which makes a man a poor leader (Is 28:7; 56:11-12) and which disrupts the life of the community of which he is a part. The daughter is guilty of unchastity. Her primary offense is the failure to preserve her sexuality for her future husband, just as her primary function in life is to marry and bear children for her husband.

The difference in status is also reflected in the inheritance practices presupposed by the Deuteronomic family legislation. The law of levirate marriage (Deut 25:5-10) seems to exclude the possibility of daughters inheriting. We have argued that the purpose of the law of levirate marriage was to provide an heir for the deceased man in order to establish his name, and that the heir must be a son. Levirate marriage would be prescribed in the case where a man had died leaving daughters, but no sons, as well as the case where a man had no children.[23]

Thus, the laws assume that sons may look forward to inheriting their father's property. Daughters normally will not inherit. Rather, they will depend upon their husband and his household for their economic well-being.

### c. Wife: Gender Asymmetry Within Marriage

Three factors suggest the subordination of the wife to her husband: (i) male economic control, (ii) male initiative in contracting and dissolving marriage, and (iii) male possession of female sexuality and reproductive capacity.

#### i. Economic Control

The Deuteronomic legislation pays little attention to financial matters. It is therefore not surprising that the Deuteronomic family laws

---

22   The prohibitions against passing one's children through the fire include daughters as well as sons (Deut 12:31; 18:10).

23   See pp. 64-65, esp. n. 5.

for the most part ignore the monetary concerns which command so much attention in the Code of Hammurabi or the Neo-Babylonian laws. There are, however, two references or allusions to property in the Deuteronomic family laws which suggest that ideally men exercised economic control within the household.

The first is the strictly patrimonial lines of inheritance presupposed by the laws (see above). The second has to do with the payment of damages. According to Deut 22:19 and Deut 22:29, damages for slandering or violating a young woman are to be paid to her father. The damages prescribed by Deut 22:19 may be understood as compensation for slander, in which case the father receives payment for an injury to the honor of the family. Alternatively, the damages may be understood as a penalty for the groom's fraudulent attempt to recover the bridewealth which he had paid for his rejected bride, which suggests that the father typically arranged the financial aspects of his daughter's marriage. The fifty shekels paid to the father in Deut 22:29 represents the daughter's bridewealth; again the father is seen as typically responsible for the financial arrangements of his daughter's marriage. Our earlier discussion of the Neo-Babylonian material cautions us that the passages' use of the term "father" does not exclude the possibility that other family members might receive the damages, especially in the absence of the father. It does suggest that, in the Deuteronomic view, the father typically (or ideally) controls such financial matters.

Based on other biblical texts, we would expect that the father typically controls the family's resources.[24] What evidence Deuteronomy offers confirms that expectation.[25]

### ii. *Marriage and Divorce*

The second indication that Deuteronomic family law presupposes the subordination of women to their husbands is that the laws depict men as

---

24 The father or husband's veto power over women's vows set forth in Num 30, for example, implies male control over family resources. Katharine Doob Sakenfeld, in an unpublished essay, suggests that Num 30 "has very much to do with the matter of economic control, control of property, by the male heads of household."

25 This is not to suggest that Deuteronomic family law assumes that women were not able to possess property. As discussed above (pp. 80-81), it is important to distinguish between ideal or typical family patterns and actual social practices. Moreover, one must avoid negative arguments from silence. Deuteronomic family law has nothing to say about the different possible ways in which ancient Near Eastern women might come to possess property: dowries, widowhood settlements, divorce settlements, and the like. Such silence cannot be interpreted as proof that women did not receive such settlements.

The OT as a whole offers little evidence concerning women's possession of property. It is clear that in at least some periods of Israel's history women could possess valuables or property (see pp. 69-70, n. 28).

the agents and women as the objects of both marriage and divorce. After a brief general description of the pattern of marriage presupposed by the Deuteronomic family laws, we will consider the husband's rights to initiate marriage and divorce as those rights do or do not indicate the subordinate position of the wife.

As has been widely recognized, the general pattern of the formation of marriage which emerges from the Deuteronomic family laws is congruent with the pattern of formation of marriage attested throughout the ancient Near East.[26] That is, betrothal and marriage are enacted by the agent of the bride, typically her father, who gives her to the groom (or his agent), and the groom (or his agent), who takes her.[27] The groom's exclusive claim to the woman is established by betrothal or inchoate marriage (אָרַשׂ);[28] after betrothal, she is called his wife (אִשָּׁה, Deut 22:24), and the claims of the husband over her are established with reference to outsiders.[29] Sexual intercourse with her is then adultery and a capital offense (Deut 22:23-27).[30]

---

26  The formation of marriage in the ancient Near East has been the subject of a great deal of literature. See for example van Praag, *Droit Matrimonial Assyro-Babylonien*; Roth, *BMA*; and Westbrook, OBML. On marriage in ancient Israel, see Burrows, *Israelite Marriage*; David Mace, *Hebrew Marriage: A Sociological Study* (London: Epworth Press, 1953); Neufeld, *AHML*; C. R. Taber, "Marriage," *IDBSup*, 573-576.

27  Deut 22:14, 16.

28  Deuteronomic law, like other ancient Near Eastern legal and narrative materials, appears to presuppose that betrothal is normally enacted by the payment of bridewealth. The fifty shekels paid to the father in Deut 22:29 probably represents a typical bridewealth; cf. also Deut 22:19. The Hebrew verb translated "betroth" or "inchoately marry," אָרַשׂ, may also imply payment of a bridewealth. In 2 Sam 3:14, David sends for his wife Michal, on the grounds that he betrothed her to himself for one hundred Philistine foreskins: אֲרַשְׂתִּי לִי בְּמֵאָה עָרְלוֹת פְּלִשְׁתִּים. Those same foreskins are referred to as "bridewealth" (מֹהַר) in 1 Sam 18:25.
     Comparative cuneiform documents make it clear that the payment of bridewealth establishes an inchoate marriage, although that does not appear to be the only way to do so. See Westbrook, OBML, vol. 2, 66-81, and Yaron, *Laws of Eshnunna*, 172-176.

29  The betrothed girl is a "wife" as far as third parties are concerned, but not as far as her parents and betrothed husband are concerned. The cuneiform codes indicate that the agents of the bride and groom could still break the contract at this point, though they would have to pay a penalty. Judg 15:2 and 1 Sam 18:19 suggest that the father could break the betrothal in Israel also. See Westbrook, OBML, vol. 2, 66-73.

30  The law of levirate marriage, at least, seems to presuppose that the bride's obligation is to the *bêt āb*. A woman appears to be subject to levirate obligations (1) if her father-in-law is still alive (Gen 38), or (2) if her deceased husband and his brother(s) had maintained a single household (Deut 25:5-10). That is, if her husband were not the head of his household, her obligation would be to his family and would continue beyond his death. If he were the head of his own household, her obligation would cease with his death.

The fact that the young woman is typically the object, not the agent, of her first marriage reflects at a very general level the patriarchal character of the society assumed by the Deuteronomic laws.[31] It provides little if any assistance, however, in determining the status of women presupposed by Deuteronomic law relative to the status of women presupposed by other biblical or cuneiform codes. The number and kinds of restrictions placed on women within the various ancient Near Eastern cultures appears to have varied widely. All of the codes, however, depict women as typically the objects of their first marriages.[32]

The man's right to initiate divorce may be more indicative of the status of women presupposed by Deuteronomic family law. Deuteronomic family law contains two pieces of evidence that indicate that a man could easily obtain a divorce from his wife. First, the first verse of the law prohibiting the restoration of marriage (Deut 24:1-4), אִם־לֹא תִמְצָא־חֵן בְּעֵינָיו כִּי־מָצָא בָהּ עֶרְוַת דָּבָר, "if she found no favor in his eyes because he has found some indecency in her," has long been interpreted as evidence of the grounds upon which a man might obtain a divorce. While it is probably not possible to determine the meaning of the crux, עֶרְוַת דָּבָר, with any precision, we have argued that the phrase cannot signify a serious offense.[33]

Second, the Deuteronomic family laws twice prohibit a man from ever divorcing a wife whom he has injured (Deut 22:19 and 22:29). Although these prohibitions are not frequently cited in relationship to a man's

---

31   That the young woman was the object, not the subject of her first marriage may well have to do with her age. Roth, "Age at Marriage," 737, concludes that the average age of an Assyrian or Babylonian woman entering into her first marriage would be between fourteen and twenty. We may assume Israelite women would enter into marriage at comparable ages. Roth also presents evidence that the groom's father served as his agent if he was still alive. Roth concludes that the average age for men entering into their first marriage was between twenty-six and thirty-two. It was therefore less likely that the groom's father would still be living.

The discrepancy between the age of the wife and the husband at the time of marriage, however, is itself evidence of the patriarchal structure of the society. The man presumably marries later than the woman because he generally must wait either until he inherits his share of the patrimony or until he acquires the means to support a family in some other way. Economic control is in the hands of the male head of the household.

The law of the restoration of marriage suggests that a woman was competent to enter into a second marriage on her own behalf (Deut 24:2).

32   Moreover, for a woman to be the agent of her own marriage was not necessarily a mark of high status. In three Neo-Babylonian marriage contracts where the woman serves as her own agent, there is no indication that the woman has a particularly high social status (Roth, BMA, 39-40; 89-90; 98). Also, the marriage contract of a highly placed woman of Elephantine, one Mivṭaḥiah, who appears to be on equal footing with her husband, still names her father as her agent (Yaron, Aramaic Papyri, 45).

33   See pp. 57, n. 44.

freedom to divorce his wife, they nonetheless actually provide evidence that is less ambiguous than Deut 24:1. The prohibitions are to be understood as a penalty for slandering or raping the young woman. It is unlikely that the force of the penalty would be to require the man to remain married to the woman even if she committed a serious offense; it is also unlikely that the penalty would prohibit the man from doing something that it would be extremely difficult for him to do in any case. The weight of the penalty depends upon it prohibiting the man from acquiring a divorce that he otherwise might readily obtain. These verses, then, support the view that Deuteronomic family law presupposes that a man was relatively free to divorce his wife.[34]

The Deuteronomic family laws are silent about possible divorce payments. The financial arrangements for marriage are outside of the purview of Deuteronomic, and, in fact, biblical law.

The Deuteronomic laws are also silent about whether women ever had the right to initiate divorce. The one small piece of evidence concerning a woman's right to dissolve her marital obligations is negative. The law of levirate marriage (Deut 25:5-10) presupposes that the woman could not sever levirate obligations at will. If her brother-in-law refused to fulfill his levirate obligations, the woman had to go to the elders and the elders had to hear him declare his refusal to marry her before she was freed from her levirate obligation. It seems unlikely, given the overall picture of women presented by the Deuteronomic laws, that the wife could initiate divorce; however, there is not enough evidence to be conclusive.

### iii. *Male Possession of Female Sexuality*

The third indication that the Deuteronomic family laws presuppose the wife's subordination to her husband is the fact that the laws view the wife's sexuality and reproductive capacity as the exclusive possession of her husband, not of herself. This view of women's sexuality, which obtains throughout the Old Testament, is correctly stated by Mace. He writes that the Old Testament regards "the woman's sexuality as the property of the man under whose *potestas* she was. In the case of her father, this involved

---

34  A. Toeg, "Does Deut 24:1-4 Incorporate a General Law on Divorce?" *Dine Israel* 2 (1970): 13, asserts that Deut 22:19 and 29 are "obvious exceptions which prove the general rule...that the husband was otherwise free to divorce his wife at his will." Toeg also points to the late prophetical "tirade" against divorce (Mal 2:10-16) and to two similes referring to Israel as a woman who had been divorced but would now be reclaimed (Is 50:1; 54:6) as evidence of the ease with which an Israelite man might obtain a divorce. These passages at least indicate that divorce was seen as highly negative for the woman.

the exclusive right of disposal; in the case of her husband, the exclusive right of use."[35]

That this view of women's sexuality is presupposed by the Deuteronomic family laws is most apparent when one considers the laws' asymmetrical definition of adultery, and especially their asymmetrical treatment of rape.

The aim of the sexual offense laws of Deut 22:13-29 is often explained in terms of protection of the intimacy of marriage.[36] Such an explanation fails to account for the asymmetry of the Deuteronomic definition of adultery. That is, the man has an exclusive claim to his wife's sexuality; violation of that claim is a capital offense. The woman has no reciprocal claim to her husband's fidelity. The sexual offense laws, therefore, must be understood in the first place as protecting the rights of the husband.

That these rights are tantamount to possession seems clear from the Deuteronomic treatment of rape. According to Deut 22:23-27, the rape of a betrothed girl, like sexual intercourse with a consenting married woman, was a capital offense. In contrast, the rape of an unbetrothed girl (Deut 22:28-29) is a relatively minor injury.[37] The woman's marital status, not her consent or lack thereof, determines the gravity of the offense. This makes sense only if the laws presuppose that the woman's sexuality is her husband's property, not her own. Sexual violation of a married woman is a grave violation of her husband's claims.

The assumption that the husband possesses his wife's sexuality and reproductive capacity attests to the general patriarchal character of the Deuteronomic view of the family. It does not help to differentiate the Deuteronomic view of the family or women's roles within the family from the view of the family found in other ancient Near Eastern documents. The husband's exclusive claim over his wife's sexuality obtains throughout the ancient Near East.

One must also note that to say the wife's sexuality and reproductive capacity was the property of her husband is not to say that the wife was the property of her husband. The wife had rights apart from her sexuality, including rights not to be sold, and not to be falsely condemned and executed (Deut 21:14; 22:25-27).[38]

Our examination of the Deuteronomic view of mothers and daughters found ways in which they were perceived as equal to fathers and sons, and

---

35    Mace, *Hebrew Marriage*, 227.

36    This is the view of Miller, *Deuteronomy*, 163.

37    The injury is primarily to the father who stands to lose the bridewealth. The penalty, which requires the violator to marry the girl and prohibits him from ever divorcing her, shows that the girl also is recognized as an injured party. The injury, however, is that her chances of marriage and thus of social and economic security are greatly reduced, not that she has been sexually assaulted.

38    Ex 21:7-11 suggests that wives also had rights to be provided with food and shelter.

ways in which they were accorded a subordinate status. An examination of the respective rights of wives and husbands uncovers only evidence of the wives' subordination to their husbands. This is not surprising. The status of the mother is defined primarily in terms of her offspring; that of a daughter, primarily in terms of her parents. One would not expect the rights and obligations of mothers and daughters to be defined wholly in terms of gender, but also in terms of the subordination of children to their parents. The status of the wife, on the other hand, is defined by her relationship to her husband. Comparing the status of the wife with that of the husband has wholly to do with gender--and thus with the subordination of women.

### 3. The Extent of the Head of Household's Authority

The authority of the father or husband over his children or wife is not unlimited.[39] Wives and children are subject to the laws of the community, not only to the mandates of the male head-of-household. If they break these laws, they are tried and punished according to the judicial processes of the community. The Deuteronomic concern for due process is seen in the law of the rebellious son (Deut 21:18-21).[40] It is also reflected in the passages which protect an innocent woman from slander (Deut 22:13-19)[41] or execution (Deut 22:25-27).

Moreover, Deuteronomic family law presupposes that dependents within the household have certain customary rights. The first-born son has specific inheritance rights expressed by the phrase מִשְׁפַּט הַבְּכֹרָה,

---

39  The authority of the father over his offspring and that of a husband over his wife are not equivalent. There are no laws which directly assert that authority of the husband over his wife; no commandment to "honor thy husband." Both very early texts (e.g., Ex 21:7-11) and post-exilic texts (e.g., Neh 5:5) attest to the extensive powers of the father or, in his absence, the mother (2 Kgs 4:1) to dispose of their children, particularly their daughter. They may arrange for her marriage or sell her. The Deuteronomic laws presuppose that the husband has no power to sell his wife. If he is tired of her, he must divorce her.

40  This concern for due process is found in several other Deuteronomic texts, including Deut 17:2-7, 8-13; 19:15-21.

41  Locher, Die Ehre Einer Frau, 373-380, holds that Deuteronomy does not treat false charges brought against a woman (Deut 22:19) as seriously as it treats false charges brought against a man (Deut 19:16-19). He argues that the husband who falsely charges his wife with unchastity is not subject to the same penalty which she would suffer if she were guilty. If that were true, one would have to conclude that the passage actually denied due process to women.

The discrepancy between Deut 19:16-19 and Deut 22:19, however, is better understood as reflecting the difference between the penalty for testifying falsely in court and the penalty for slanderous talk in the community. (The discrepancy between CH 127, ANET, 171, and CH 3, ANET, 166, is to be understood in the same way.)

"customary rights of the first-born son" (Deut 21:17).[42] A wife has the
right not to be sold (Deut 21:14).[43]

The laws that seek to protect the rights of dependents acknowledge
the authority of the father or husband even as they seek to limit that
authority. The Deuteronomic family laws consistently regulate the
behavior of those with power in a given situation, rather than directly
asserting the rights of dependents. Usually the one whose behavior is
addressed is the male head of household.[44] Twice, the laws regulate the
behavior of the father and the mother.[45] Once, a law addresses the
behavior of the wife of a deceased man, who is to act in a representative
capacity on behalf of her dead husband.[46] That the laws are primarily
concerned with the behavior of the male heads of households is an
indication of the authority exercised by those men.

The law of primogeniture and the law of the rebellious son most
clearly recognize both the authority of the father and the limits to that
authority. The law of primogeniture insists that the father shall recognize
the rights of the chronologically first-born: כִּי אֶת־הַבְּכֹר בֶּן־הַשְּׂנוּאָה יַכִּיר
(Deut 21:17). The verb translated "recognize," נכר, is a technical legal
term. The phrase suggests that the father had to acknowledge the rights
of the son in order for the son to claim them.[47] We have also argued that
the courts may not have been able to act against an incorrigible son
unless his parents surrendered him.

## 4. Conclusions

In conclusion, the authority of the male head of household was not
unlimited. Dependent family members were not subject to the private
justice of their father or husband. Rather, both the male head of the

---

42   A similar phrase found in Ex 21:9, מִשְׁפַּט הַבָּנוֹת, suggests that daughters and
     daughters-in-law also had certain customary rights.
43   The thrust of the second part of the law of the captive bride (Deut 21:14) is that the
     captive woman now has the status of a wife. The law *presupposes* that wives can not
     be sold.
44   Deut 21:10-14, 15-17; 24:1-4; 25:5.
45   Deut 21:18-21; 22:13-19.
46   Deut 25:7-10. The family laws also seek to regulate the behavior of the elders (Deut
     22:18; 25:8) and the men responsible for stoning the rebellious son or unchaste bride
     (Deut 21:21; 22:21, 22, 24, 26).
47   David Daube, *Studies in Biblical Law* (New York: Ktav Publishing House, 1969),
     5-10; Zeev Falk, *Hebrew Law in Biblical Times* (Jerusalem: Wahrmann Books,
     1964), 168.
         Contrast the wording of Deut 21:15-17 with that wording of MAL B:1, *ANET*,
     185, which regulates the sons' actions rather than the father's: "[the eldest son] shall
     choose (and) take two portions [as his share], and his brothers one after the other
     shall choose (and) take (their portions)" (Driver and Miles, *AL*, 427).

household and the dependent family members were subject to the judicial processes of the community. The interests of dependent family members were guarded by certain customary rights as well as by injunctions whose purpose was to protect vulnerable persons.

Nonetheless, the laws clearly do presuppose that the authority of the male head of the household was extensive. This is seen in the laws intended to curb abuses of his powers as well as in the laws aimed at asserting the interests of the man.

The laws assume that women are dependent upon a male headed family for their economic and social welfare. Within that family, the laws assume that the woman has a subordinate status, whether she is mother, daughter, or wife. The woman achieves a status most equal to that of her male counterpart in her role as mother. That parity is found only in relationship to her offspring, however, and only in relationship to intrafamily matters. That same woman in her role as wife is subject to her husband. He has the unilateral power to initiate or terminate marriage; his claims over her sexuality are unilateral and absolute, and he exerts control over the economics of the family.

# Chapter Six: Overall Purpose
## of the Deuteronomic Family Laws

### 1. *Introduction*

Chapter 5 argues that the Deuteronomic family laws presuppose the dependent status of women within the family. That is, Deuteronomic law takes for granted that a woman's social legitimacy and economic security depend on her status within a male headed household. The laws also take for granted the subordination of women within the family. The woman--as mother, daughter, or wife--will have a more restricted and less powerful role than her male counterparts of father, son, or husband.

Chapter 6 will examine the overall purpose of these laws as that purpose relates to the status of women within the family. It would be quite possible for the laws to presuppose the subordinate status of women, but to aim at altering that status. For example, Deut 21:14 presupposes that a captive woman married to an Israelite man would be extremely vulnerable; it seeks to protect such captives from the most brutal consequences (enslavement) of their vulnerability. We must therefore ask not only what familial structures are presupposed by the Deuteronomic laws, but also whether the main thrust of the laws is to undergird or to change those family structures.

The question is sharpened by the fact that a number of scholars believe that the Deuteronomic laws seek to promote the equality of women and men. Weinfeld, for example, states that "Deuteronomy shows a particularly humanistic attitude towards women," an attitude which endorsed "the equality of the sexes."[1] Naomi Steinberg uses the Deuteronomic family laws to support her thesis that men enjoyed no "advantage" in comparison to women within the Israelite family. "Consistently the legislation in Deuteronomy 19-25 reflects an attempt to preserve the social standing of women against the willfulness of men." She believes that this Deuteronomic effort to restrain the willfulness of men emphatically demonstrates that "the sexes are not ranked hierarchically within the family setting."[2] Phillips believes that bringing women into "full membership in the covenant community" was one of the two main innovations of the Deuteronomic reform.[3]

---

1    Weinfeld, *DDS*, 291. Weinfeld argues that this "particularly humanistic view toward women" is a result of the influence of the school of wisdom on the Deuteronomic author, and presents the Deuteronomic treatment of women as evidence that Deuteronomy emerged from scribal circles.

2    Steinberg, "Adam's and Eve's Daughters," 275, 279.

3    Phillips, *AICL*, 180; Rémy, "La Condition de la femme," 296-299; and Goldingay,

In contrast, we will argue that the Deuteronomic family laws support the hierarchical and patrilineal structures of the family. They are essentially conservative. In fact, the laws serve a two-fold purpose. In the first place, they undergird the traditional structures of the family, the interests of which are, for the most part, identified with the interests of the male head of the household. In the second place, the laws protect the rights of dependent family members. They do so, however, without challenging the subordinate status of women in any fundamental way.[4] In our opinion, and in contrast to Steinberg's thesis, the Deuteronomic laws both presuppose and undergird hierarchical family relationships between the sexes.

## 2. *The Support of Hierarchical, Patrilineal Family Structures in the Deuteronomic Family Laws*

The primary thrust of the Deuteronomic family laws is, simply, to promote the stability of the family. The family which Deuteronomy promotes, as elsewhere in the ancient Near East, is hierarchically structured, with a male head of household. It is patrilineal and patrimonial; that is, it is defined in terms of male lineage and the land handed down from father to son. In the Deuteronomic law, the interests of the family and the interests of the male head of the family are in large measure identical.[5] The Deuteronomic concerns for the family may be discussed under the rubrics (a) order, (b) integrity, and (c) continuity.

---

*Theological Diversity*, 138, also hold that Deuteronomic law is especially concerned with the welfare of women.

4   Rofé, "Family and Sex Laws," 131-160, also notes that the purpose of these laws has two dimensions. He ascribes them, however, to different literary strata. Deut 21:18-21 and 22:20-21 are supposed to belong to a later and more conservative redactional layer. Rofé describes the intention of these laws as an effort "to halt the erosion of family values such as chastity or filial obedience .... The legal means by which the writer proposes to achieve his aim indicate how very removed he is from the type of patriarchal system he wishes to reinstate" ("Family and Sex Laws," 145).
     The Deuteronomic concerns on the one hand to uphold traditional family structures and on the other to protect dependent family members are, however, both found within the same laws. For example, Deut 22:28-29 has to do with both the father's right to the bridewealth and control over his daughter's sexuality, and with securing social status and economic security for the girl. Moreover, this law is, in its final form, thoroughly integrated with the section which begins with Deut 22:13 and concludes with Deut 22:29, the major thrust of which is to emphasize the gravity of violating a father's or husband's control over the sexuality of his daughter or wife. The final editors of the laws must have held both concerns.

5   Bird describes biblical law in a way that is clearly apropos of Deuteronomic family legislation. She writes: "One of the chief aims of Israelite law is to assure the integrity, stability and economic viability of the family as the basic unity of society. In this legislation, however, the interests of the family are commonly identified with those of its male head" ("Images of Women," 51).

These concerns may equally be described as (a) parental and especially paternal authority, and male control over female sexuality; (b) again, male control of female sexuality; and (c) a man's right to have sons.

### a. Order

The Deuteronomic laws support the family by undergirding family order, that is, the structures of authority and control within the family. The Deuteronomic laws assert the authority of the parents, and the control of the husband over his wife.

Two laws emphasize the inviolability of parental authority. As was previously discussed, Deut 21:18-21, the law of the rebellious son, emphasizes the gravity of the son's offense and the sacredness of the parents' authority; it does not aim at limiting the father's powers.[6] The law of the unchaste bride (Deut 22:20-21) also severely sanctions violation of the father's authority.[7] The motive clause of the law underscores that in the Deuteronomic view the girl's offense is against her father. She has "fornicated while under the authority of her father," לִזְנוֹת בֵּית אָבִיהָ. That she is to be executed outside the door of her father's household also emphasizes that her behavior has violated the honor and authority of her father.[8] The severity of the punishment stresses the gravity of the offense.

The husband's unilateral control over his wife's sexuality is forcefully asserted in the adultery laws (Deut 22:13-29).[9] Scholars debate the rationale behind the strict biblical prohibition of adultery; no explicit rationale for the prohibition is given in the Bible. It seems likely that the horror of the offense was considered self-evident. Adultery was the "great sin."[10] The wickedness of the offense was apparently more obvious than

---

6    See pp. 17-19.

7    A discussion of similarities between the two laws is found on p. 85, n. 21.

8    Phillips interprets the site of the girl's execution as a sign of the father's culpability: "This takes place ... outside her father's house as a sign of community displeasure over his fraud, whether or not he was aware of the facts" (*Deuteronomy*, 149). Elsewhere in ancient Near Eastern laws and legal documents, however, an extraordinary site of execution reflects either the nature of the offense or the victim, not a co-offender (see CH 21, *ANET*, 167; CH 25, *ANET*, 167; CH 256, *ANET*, 177; HL 166, *ANET*, 195). A homicide trial, 2N-t.54, is studied by Thorkild Jacobsen, "An Ancient Mesopotamian Trial for Homicide," in *Toward the Image of Tammuz and Other Essays on Mesopotamian history and Culture*, ed. William L. Moran (Cambridge: Harvard University Press, 1970), 193-214. In that trial, the guilty parties are sentenced to be killed "before the chair" of their victim.

9    To be sure, the husband's control over his wife's sexuality is not equivalent to the father and mother's authority over their son. The latter has to do with the right to demand obedience, the former to do with possession and the right to require fidelity. Nonetheless, both have to do with control, and with family order.

10   Gen 20:9. According to William L. Moran, "The Scandal of the 'Great Sin' at Ugarit," *JNES* 18 (1959): 280-281; and Jacob J. Rabinowitz, "The 'Great Sin' in

the wickedness of idolatry, for adultery could be used metaphorically to move people to recognize the evil of idolatry. Presumably violating a man's possession of his wife's sexuality was experienced as a fundamental wrong which required no rationale.[11] Modern attempts to articulate the rationale underlying the laws are, therefore, somewhat artificial.

Nonetheless, we may assume that the laws prohibiting adultery have to do, in part, with the husband's control over his household, and thus with family order. At the same time, they forcefully assert the interests of the husband.

### b. *Integrity*

The Deuteronomic laws also undergird family integrity, both in the sense of unity and in the sense of biological purity. The laws which control women's sexuality have to do not only with lines of power and authority and thus with family order but also with maintaining the integrity of the boundaries of the family.

Frymer-Kensky rightly states that biblical law keenly recognizes the double-edged power of sexuality to create and to shatter family relationships: "These laws of control reveal a sense that sexuality is ... a two-edged sword: a force for bonding and a threat to the maintenance of boundaries."[12] Frymer-Kensky notes, but unfortunately does not stress, that the biblical laws are primarily concerned with controlling the sexuality of women. In her view, this asymmetry stems from the fact "that for a man to sleep with a woman who belonged to some other household threatened the definition of 'household' and 'family'; for a married man to sleep with an unattached woman is not mentioned as an item of concern."[13]

---

Ancient Egyptian Marriage Contracts," *JNES* 18 (1959): 73, adultery was also called the "great sin" in Ugarit and Egypt.

11    The biblical laws apparently share this perception of the fundamental nature of the offense with nearly all ancient law codes. Daniel Murray, "Ancient Laws on Adultery--A Synopsis," *Journal of Family Law* 1 (1961): 89-104, surveys ancient prohibitions against adultery in the Middle East, Far East, Greece, Rome, England, Ireland, Scotland, Wales, and the Germanic codes. He finds that adultery was nearly universally treated as a most grave crime (the exception is Sparta). It was universally asymmetrically defined as a violation of the husband's rights over his wife, and not of the wife's rights over her husband. Murray writes that the laws suggest a variety of reasons behind the prohibition of adultery, including violation of the community's moral sense, threat to the integrity of the family, and the man's property rights over his wife's body. He concludes, however, that the "tacit underlying reason in all legal systems was that adultery was a blow to a man's pride; another was considered superior in *l'amour*" (89).

12    Frymer-Kensky, "Law and Philosophy," 98.

13    Ibid., 92. Frymer-Kensky argues that the asymmetrical treatment of sexual offenses is part of Israel's inheritance from the surrounding cultures, which it adopted unthinkingly. It seems more likely that the Deuteronomic redactors intended to

The asymmetrical character of the adultery laws should be stressed. If, as Frymer-Kensky correctly states, for a married woman to sleep with anyone other than her husband fundamentally "threatened the definition of family" but for a married man to sleep with an unmarried woman posed no such threat, it is because the family was defined in terms of the male. Because the man defines the family, the family unit can tolerate his having liaisons with more than one woman and still be a single family. It cannot tolerate the woman having liaisons with more than one man; she would then be part of two different families and the boundaries defining each household would disintegrate.

Moreover, if lineage is defined in terms of the father, then he must be certain that his children are his own. The woman has the potential to adulterate his lineage. The biological integrity of his family depends upon his exclusive possession of his wife's (or wives') sexuality.

Thus, the asymmetrical adultery laws support the integrity of the family, but only because the family is defined in terms of the male head of household. The interests of the family are understood in terms of the man's interests.

The rather odd law found in Deut 25:11-12 is also indirectly concerned with the integrity of the family. The law prescribes punishment for a woman who has seized the genitals of a man who was fighting with her husband. According to this law, even if she acted in defense of her husband the judges are to cut off her hand. Several rationales have been suggested for this law. The most likely one interprets the woman's act as a severe breach of modesty. That is, sexual contact between a married woman and a man other than her husband is absolutely forbidden. That the woman's act is punished so severely even under the most extenuating circumstances emphasizes the gravity of the offense of a married woman initiating sexual contact with another man. Thus this law also undergirds the husband's strict claim over his wife's sexuality. Despite the fact that the law punishes a woman for an act committed in defense of her husband, it indirectly supports her husband's claims over her by emphasizing the gravity of any breach of the sexual laws on the part of the woman.[14]

---

undergird the man's claims to his wife's sexuality and to emphasize the seriousness of the offense. We have argued that in practice an Israelite man whose wife committed adultery probably could have imposed upon her a range of penalties including pardon or divorce, or he could have demanded the death penalty. If that is the case, then the Deuteronomic mandate of the death penalty for adultery and the accompanying expurgation formula indicate the gravity with which the Deuteronomic redactors viewed the offense. A man's claims to his wife's sexuality were inviolable. The claims, moreover, were retroactive (Deut 22:20-21). Sexual contact between a married woman and a man other than her husband was inexcusable even under the most extenuating circumstances (Deut 25:11-12).

14  "Breach of modesty" is the rationale for the law proposed by Paul, "Analogues,"

We have argued that Deuteronomy 24:1-4 also has to do with the integrity of the patrilineal family. This law prohibits the remarriage of a man to a woman whom he had divorced if in the meantime she had been married and divorced or widowed. The law is to be understood by analogy to adultery; relationships between a woman and first one man, then a second, and then again the first violated the Deuteronomic understanding of sexual purity. The remarriage would pollute the land. We have suggested that this purity belief is a matter of maintaining boundaries. The clarity of the boundaries between one family and another would be blurred by such crisscrossing relationships.[15] The prohibition does not directly serve either the first or second husband's interests; indeed, it actually limits the prerogatives of the first husband. It does support the integrity of the patrilineal family.[16]

### c. Continuity

Finally, the Deuteronomic family laws support the male-headed family by seeking to ensure the continuity of the family through the male line. This is most clearly visible in the law of levirate marriage (Deut 25:5-10). The aim of this law is explicitly stated: the purpose of the levirate union is to provide a son for the man who died without an heir, in order to establish the dead man's name. While the meaning of "name" is elusive, it most likely refers to the man's ongoing household or lineage. Establishing the man's name has to do with ensuring that his descendants continue to possess his land.[17] The law protects the family by seeking to assure its continuity.

---

333-350; Patrick, *Old Testament Law*, 138-39; Daube, "The Culture of Deuteronomy," 27-52; and Weinfeld, *DDS*, 292.

Oddly enough, Weinfeld takes the difference between the Assyrian law (which punishes a woman for physically injuring a man's genitals by cutting off one finger) and the Deuteronomic law (which punishes a woman for touching a man's genitals by cutting off her hand) as an indication of the Deuteronomic author's humane view of women. That is, he views the shift in focus of the law from physical injury to sexual modesty as progressive. His interpretation is strained.

Deut 25:11-12 is discussed in more detail, pp. 74-77.

15   See pp. 60-61.

16   Deuteronomy 21:10-13, the law of the captive bride, undergirds the integrity of the family in a somewhat different sense. Its primary purpose seems to be to provide the man with an alternative legal way to marry a woman in a situation where the normal contractual means of effecting a marriage are not possible. The ritual actions prescribed for the captive woman and the thirty day mourning period suggest a second purpose of the law. The rituals and the waiting period clearly demarcate the woman's new life as a member of an Israelite household from her pre-Israelite life. The law thus helps the foreigner to be assimilated, and so protects the boundaries of an Israelite household from the threat which her foreignness may represent.

17   See pp. 66-68.

The primary interests served by the law, however, are the interests of the deceased. For a man's name to be established was vital to the meaning of his existence. It is quite likely that it was considered necessary to his continued existence after death.[18] Again the interests of the family coincide with the interests of the male head of household.

Concern for the continuity of the family and for a man's right to an heir probably also underlies the one year exemption from military or other state service granted to a newly married man in Deut 24:5.[19] The wording of the law in its received form emphasizes the enjoyment of life's pleasures: וְשִׂמַּח אֶת־אִשְׁתּוֹ אֲשֶׁר־לָקָח, "he shall rejoice with (or give joy to) his wife whom he has taken."[20] Such an exemption, however, would surely increase the chances that the couple would bear a son to continue the family.

### d. Summary

The Deuteronomic family laws examined have as their primary focus neither women, per se, nor men, per se, but the family. They support the family, however, by affirming parental and especially paternal authority, by asserting the husband's unilateral and exclusive claims over his wife's

---

18   McBride, "Deuteronomic Name Theology," esp. 77-117, identifies a belief common to the ancient Near East that the name of a man participates in his reality. The name is a semi-hypostasis. By preserving his name, a man's son perpetuates his very existence. McBride cautions that the phrase "establish his name" in Deut 25:5-10 may be simply a cliché rather than a reflection of Deuteronomic mortuary beliefs. Alternatively, McBride suggests that the Deuteronomic authors may have incorporated the levirate law as part of their polemic against the high places. That is, a man's name was to be perpetuated by his sons, not by a mortuary stela (100).

As has been shown in the exegesis (pp. 66-69), the passage places a good deal of emphasis on the use of the term "name." It is repeated twice in Deut 25:6-7 and further stressed by the mirror punishment imposed upon a man who fails to raise up his brother's name; he shall be given a shameful name. Such stress on the concept "name" makes it unlikely that it is simply a cliché. The centrality of the theologumenon "establishing God's name" in Deuteronomy also makes it seem unlikely that the Deuteronomic compilers would unthinkingly pass on the phrase "establish his name" in a clichéd manner.

19   Deut 20:7 similarly exempts from battle a betrothed man who has not yet married his wife.

20   Weinfeld, DDS, 291, believes that the law demonstrates the Deuteronomic redactors' "consideration for a woman's intimate feelings." This assertion is problematic. The consonantal text is ambiguous at a critical point. It reads: ושמח אֶת־אִשְׁתּוֹ אֲשֶׁר־לָקָח. שמח can be taken as a piel stem and את as the sign of the direct object, in which case the phrase could be translated "to give joy to the wife he has taken." The verb could also be taken as a qal stem, and את could be understood as the preposition "with." The phrase would then be translated "to be happy with his wife whom he has taken." The NRSV adopts the latter translation. The MT and Targum Onkelos point שמח in the piel stem; the Vulgate and Targum Jonathan reflect the alternative tradition.

sexuality, and by addressing a man's need for a male heir. In these laws, the interests of the family are largely identified with the interests of the man.

In some of the specific laws, the interests of the woman are either explicitly included (the authority of the mother is asserted along with the authority of the father) or coincide with the interests of the man (the wife of the deceased husband benefits from bearing his heir). Elsewhere the laws clearly oppose the interests of the woman (as, for example, in the asymmetrical character of Deut 22:20-24 and 25:11-12). Taken as a whole these laws serve to reinforce the subordinate status of women by undergirding existing structures of authority, and by reinforcing existing definitions of the family as male-centered.

### 3. Protection of Dependent Family Members

The Deuteronomic family laws not only support the authority of the dominant family members, they also extend protection to dependent family members. They do so within the context of a hierarchically structured family.

The first two family laws found in Deuteronomy (Deut 21:10-14 and 21:15-17) explicitly limit the prerogatives of the male and protect the rights of dependent family members. The captive woman taken as a bride cannot be reenslaved and sold. The phrase לֹא־תִתְעַמֵּר בָּהּ, which may be translated "you have no power to sell her,"[21] stresses the limitation placed on the husband's power over his wife, while the motive clause תַּחַת אֲשֶׁר עִנִּיתָהּ, "because you have had your way with her" recognizes the injury done to the woman taken captive.[22] Deut 21:15-17 limits the father's ability to dispose of his possessions; he may not arbitrarily transfer the birthright from his chronologically first-born son. The final law in that set asserts the parents' authority over their son. Thus, in the three laws, existing structures of authority are supported, but limitations on that authority are also affirmed.[23] This set of laws exemplifies the pattern of asserting and limiting authority found throughout the Deuteronomic family laws.

The protections which the laws offer to women fall into two main categories. First, the laws provide social legitimacy and economic security to women who are particularly vulnerable for various reasons. Second,

---

21    Following Alt. See p. 14, n. 16.

22    See pp. 14-15.

23    This pattern of affirming existing structures of control but protecting the rights of dependents is also found in the sexual offense laws. The primary thrust of these laws is to assert the claims of the husband and protect the integrity of the family. The laws incorporate protection of the slandered bride, the raped betrothed girl, and the raped virgin.

the laws protect innocent dependent family members from false accusation and execution.

### a. *Social Legitimacy and Economic Security*

As we have seen, Deut 21:10-14 secures the status of "wife" for the captive woman whom a man has chosen to marry. Once she is his wife, that status cannot be taken from her; she may not be reenslaved and sold.

Two laws mandate reparative marriage for an injured woman. Deut 22:19 requires that a man who has slandered his bride must maintain her as a wife. He may never divorce her. Similarly, Deut 22:29 requires a man who rapes a woman to marry her and prohibits him from ever divorcing her. In both of these cases, the woman would otherwise be in a precarious position. The slandered woman was dishonored; it might be difficult for her family to find her another husband. The raped girl was probably made unmarriageable by the violation; at the least, her chances of marriage were greatly injured.[24] The man who injured her was obligated to provide for her economic support, and to offer her a legitimate place in society. These stipulations may have served the interests of the woman's father as well as the interests of the woman. Presumably if the slanderous husband or the rapist did not provide for the injured woman, that responsibility would fall to the woman's father. Nonetheless, the laws do obtain security for the woman.

The law of levirate marriage (Deut 25:5-10) also seeks to provide security and status for a vulnerable woman by marriage. The first purpose of the law is to serve the interests of the deceased man by the establishment of his name. The law also serves to protect a childless widow by providing her with a husband and a son.[25]

---

24    Virginity is not a prerequisite for marriage; according to the Deuteronomic family laws, a widow or divorcee could certainly remarry (Deut 24:1-4). There are some indications, however, that a woman who had been defiled by illicit sexual relations was not eligible for marriage. Deut 22:20-21 certainly shows that a girl was expected to be a virgin at her first marriage. 2 Sam 13:20 may also indicate that a woman who had been sexually defiled was not marriageable. 2 Sam 13:20 states that after the rape, Tamar lived שֹׁמֵמָה, as a "desolate woman"; elsewhere שֹׁמֵמָה is used in metaphors depicting Judah as an unmarried, childless woman (Is 54:1; cf. 62:4). That Tamar was rendered unmarriageable by the rape is also suggested by her statement that Amnon's rejection of her after having violated her was a greater wrong than the violation itself (v. 16). That sexually defiled women were ineligible for marital relations is also suggested by the story of David's concubines. David continued to provide for the concubines whom Absalom had defiled, but the text specifically notes that he never again had sexual relations with them (2 Sam 20:3). Finally, the phrase "defiled" in Deut 24:4 must mean that she is disqualified for further sexual relations with her former husband.

25    Perhaps because he is not responsible for having injured her, the brother of the deceased husband is not compelled to marry his sister-in-law. Rather, the law seeks

### b. *Protection from False Accusation*

Elements of two laws, Deut 22:25-27 and 21:18-21, protect dependent family members from being falsely accused and executed. First, the sexual offense laws carefully insist that a woman who has not consented to rape should not be punished. In the final form of the law, Deut 22:26-27 emphasizes the young woman's blamelessness in five different clauses.[26] The rapist alone shall die. The absence of the expurgation formula ("You shall purge the evil from your midst") in Deut 22:25-27 also indicates that these verses are more concerned with the innocence of the girl than with the guilt of the rapist.[27]

Second, the law of the rebellious son (Deut 21:18-21) reflects the Deuteronomic concern that those accused of crimes be granted due process. This is not the primary thrust of the law. In chapter 1 we argued that the primary concern of the law is to assert the authority of the parents. The explicit statement that the parents shall bring their son before the elders, together with the instructions to the parents on how to charge their son, seem to reflect a concern of the Deuteronomic redactors for fair judicial procedures.[28]

Although the law of the slandered bride (Deut 22:13-19) is most often interpreted as providing the young woman protection from being falsely accused of a capital offense, it is doubtful that this law views the husband as the plaintiff. Rather, it is the parents who bring the case before the elders, charging the husband with slander. Deut 22:13-19, then, has to do with protecting the woman and her family from slander and dishonor, rather than protecting her from false charges.

---

to shame him into fulfilling his obligations.

Deut 25:5-10 is often contrasted with Gen 38 to show how the law of the levirate became less binding over time. Onan was compelled to marry Tamar; Deut 25:7-10 allows the brother-in-law to refuse to play the role of levir. Based on this comparison, some scholars suggest that the Deuteronomic law was intended to alleviate the levir's responsibility.

This argument is based on an inaccurate reading of Gen 38. The fact that Onan's father has commanded him to raise up children for his deceased brother is a sufficient reason for the story to condemn his failure to comply. He disobeyed his father. If custom or law had actually compelled the deceased man's brother to marry the widow, Tamar would have been able to appeal to that law to obtain her rights. The fact that she resorts to such a risky way of obtaining a son for Er implies that she could not appeal to the law.

26  See p. 33, n. 33.
27  The expurgation formula is found in each of the other laws that call for the death penalty for adultery: Deut 22:21, 22, 24.
28  A similar concern for just procedures is found, for example, in Deut 17:2-7: "Upon the word of two or three witnesses, the one who is to die shall be put to death. He shall not be put to death upon the word of one witness" (v. 6). The overall purpose of the law is to emphasize the gravity of the offense of idolatry, and to motivate the community to carry out the death penalty against idolators.

## c. *Summary*

The Deuteronomic family laws do carefully show that the authority of the male head of the household is not unlimited, and that dependent family members have rights. Moreover, in four cases the laws seek to secure social status and/or economic security for women who are injured or particularly vulnerable. Finally, Deuteronomic concern for fair judicial procedures extends to Deuteronomic treatment of dependent family members.

These protections are consistent with the overall Deuteronomic concern for all members of society, especially those who are most vulnerable.[29] They also reflect the Deuteronomic concern for justice, a concern which Miller has called "no less characteristic of Deuteronomy than it is of the prophets."[30]

### 4. *Response to Assertions that Deuteronomic Family Law Promotes the Equality of Women and Men*

Without question, one aim of the Deuteronomic family laws is to protect the rights of dependent family members. The presence of such concern within the family laws, however, should not be taken as evidence that the Deuteronomic compilers sought the "equality" of women and men, or that they held a non-hierarchical view of the family. Previous discussion of the "Deuteronomic view of women" has tended to exaggerate the extent of concern for women found in these laws. It has done this in four ways.

First, specific laws have been interpreted as more focused on women's welfare than they actually are. The prohibition against the restoration of marriage (Deut 24:1-4), for example, is often read as protection of the wife; such a prohibition is supposed to prevent the husband from divorcing his wife hastily or to protect the woman by providing her with written evidence of having been divorced.[31] We have argued that this interpretation cannot be sustained because, among other reasons, it disregards the fact that the prohibition applies only in cases where the woman has entered into a second marriage.[32] Neither does the rhetoric of the law of the rebellious son allow us to interpret it as an effort to limit the power of the father.[33] The law of primogeniture (Deut 21:15-17) is

---

29    Deuteronomy's humanism has been frequently discussed. See, for example, Miller's section on "The Protection and Care of Others," in his *Deuteronomy*, 169-175.

30    Miller, *Deuteronomy*, 142. Securing just trial procedures is a consistent concern of the book of Deuteronomy. See especially 1:9-18; 16:18-20; 17:4-6, 8-13; 19:15-21.

31    Steinberg, "Adam's and Eve's Daughters," 260-263; Rémy, "La condition de la femme," 297; Driver, *Deuteronomy*, 269-273.

32    See pp. 51-52.

33    In contrast to the positions of Steinberg, "Adam's and Eve's Daughters," 250-255;

often interpreted as an effort to protect an unloved wife from the loss of inheritance rights.[34] The law does limit the prerogatives of the father, but it explicitly states that it does so in favor of the rights of the chronologically first-born son. The repeated reference to the loved and unloved wife in the law seems polemical; the law appears to be countering an actual situation. Presumably the father would be prohibited from arbitrarily disinheriting his chronologically first-born son in any situation.[35]

Thus, it may be seen that there is very limited attention to women's welfare. The protection extended to women by the Deuteronomic family laws is limited to these rights: a wife (though not a daughter) has the right not to be sold; neither wife nor daughter should be falsely accused nor should an innocent woman be executed; a slandered or raped woman has the right to reparative marriage.

Second, previous discussion has tended to interpret the concern of the Deuteronomic family laws for dependent family members as evidence that the redactors believed women are or should be equal to men. Steinberg sees within the laws a consistent attempt by the laws to limit the "willfulness of men." She then cites this tendency as evidence that the Deuteronomic ideal of the family was non-hierarchical.[36] Similarly, Weinfeld, enumerating laws which in his opinion either protect or include women, refers to "the equality of the sexes."[37] The fact that these laws protect dependent family members does not in any way indicate that the aim of the laws is to promote the equality of dependent family members and the male head of the household. The law of primogeniture, for example, protects the rights of a first-born son, while the next passage, the law of the rebellious son, adamantly requires that same son to obey that same father. Indeed, these protective laws are necessary precisely because family relationships were understood to be hierarchical; the weaker members were vulnerable to the stronger members.[38] Laws protecting dependent family members presuppose male authority even as they set limits upon it.

Third, there is a tendency to exaggerate the degree to which the Deuteronomic concern to protect dependent family members is innovative. Earlier biblical and cuneiform law codes also protect the rights of dependent family members. The Deuteronomic prohibition against selling a captive bride echoes the prohibition against selling a

and Rémy, "La condition de la femme," 298.

34   Weinfeld, *DDS*, 291; Rémy, "La condition de la femme," 297; Steinberg, "Adam's and Eve's Daughters," 248-249.
35   See pp. 15-17.
36   Steinberg, "Adam's and Eve's Daughters," 279.
37   Weinfeld, *DDS*, 291.
38   See pp. 82.

concubine found in the Book of the Covenant (Ex 21:7-11). The Deuteronomic affirmation of a violated girl's right to reparative marriage is a later version of a law already found in the Book of the Covenant (Ex 22:15-16 [Eng. 22:16-17]). Weinfeld argues that the version of the law concerning the violated virgin which is found in the Book of the Covenant is concerned only with the pecuniary rights of the father while the Deuteronomic version of the law (Deut 22:28-29) is concerned with the welfare of the young woman.[39] In fact, both versions of the law require the man who violated the young woman to marry her and to pay the bridewealth or its equivalent to her father; thus, both take into account the interests of the woman and the interests of the father.[40]

Fourth, scholars who assert that the Deuteronomic family laws promote non-hierarchical, equal relationships between women and men can do so only by taking the laws protecting dependent family members out of their context.[41] The protective laws are found within laws which affirm the centrality and authority of the male head of the household; they do not essentially challenge the traditional structures of authority and control. Moreover, the seriousness with which the Deuteronomic redactors viewed violations of the authority and control of dominant family members is evident in the penalties assigned to such violations and the motive clauses associated with them. Rebellion against parents, violating the father's authority or the husband's claims over his wife, and breach of modesty are the offenses which are most severely punished. All but the last offense are punished with death; they are regarded as violations of the covenant that pollute the community with criminal guilt that must be expurgated.[42] The laws protecting dependent family

---

39    Weinfeld writes, "The author of Deuteronomy ... is concerned with rectifying the moral and personal wrong committed against the maiden and not with the financial interests of the father" (*DDS*, 285).

40    The Book of the Covenant version of the law does seem to give the father more discretion than the Deuteronomic version gives him. Ex 22:15-16 allows that father to withhold his daughter from the man who violated her; the Deuteronomic version of the law does not state that the father has that option. According to Ex 22:15-16, the sum of the bridewealth must be negotiated with the father. Deut 22:28-29 sets the bridewealth at fifty shekels. It is not clear, however, that the differences reflect concern for the woman; they may represent a more general extension of state control, such as the tendency to fix prices. Moreover, the differences between the two laws may reflect changes that occurred in the long stretch of time between the Book of the Covenant and Deuteronomy. We do not know that they are Deuteronomic innovations.

41    See p. 6.

42    Offenses against the order of the family (Deut 21:18-21; 22:20-24) are held to be grave offenses against the community. The description of the unchaste behavior of the non-virgin bride, וְבָלָה בְּיִשְׂרָאֵל (Deut 22:21), explicitly deems her offense a violation against the communal order (see p. 30, n. 24). The gravity of the threat posed to the community by these offenses is indicated not only by the severity of the

members either impose lighter penalties (damages or reparative marriages) or no penalties.

This is in part due to formal considerations. Dale Patrick has delineated two types of casuistic laws: primary and remedial. Primary laws define the rights and status of certain persons, remedial laws establish penalties for violating those rights and statuses. Deuteronomic family legislation protecting dependent family members is for the most part primary law. The legislation protecting powerful family members is remedial in character. This formal distinction, however, still highlights the difference in status of the parties involved. Patrick correctly notes that remedial laws are for the most part aimed at undergirding existing structures of authority and power while primary laws serve to protect the weaker members of society.[43]

## 5. Deuteronomic Family Law and the Legal Liability of Women

Finally, we must examine the argument that a major purpose of the Deuteronomic family laws was to make women subject to the laws of their community rather than to the private justice of their husbands. Both Daube and Phillips have argued that the Deuteronomic laws were intended to change the status of women so that they would be liable to the law. Both scholars view this as a positive change for women. Daube has called the Deuteronomic adultery law a "biblical landmark in the struggle for women's rights."[44] Phillips asserts that "the Deuteronomist's

---

penalty but also by the means of carrying out the penalty. All of the men of the city (Deut 21:21; 22:21; and presumably 22:24) are to stone the offenders, because all of the city is threatened by the offense.

These offenses, moreover, are offenses against God. Deut 21:18-21 and 22:20-24 are Deuteronomic interpretations of the fifth and seventh commandments. Like murder and kidnapping, rebelling against one's parents or committing adultery violates the covenant and brings guilt upon the entire community. That these offenses are sins against the community and against God should not be taken to imply that they are not offenses against the parents or the husband. It is precisely violating parental authority or the rights of the husband which constitutes an offense against the community and against God. This is perhaps most clearly seen in the motive clause attached to the law of the unchaste bride: עָשְׂתָה וְבָלָה בְּיִשְׂרָאֵל לִזְנוֹת בֵּית אָבִיהָ וּבְעַרְתָּ הָרָע מִקִּרְבֶּךָ, "She has committed a crass disorder in Israel, to fornicate while under the authority of her father; You shall purge the evil from your midst." The offense against the community, וְבָלָה בְּיִשְׂרָאֵל, is precisely the violation of the authority of the father, לִזְנוֹת בֵּית אָבִיהָ, a sin against God that incurs guilt which the community must expurgate, וּבְעַרְתָּ הָרָע מִקִּרְבֶּךָ.

43    Dale Patrick, "Casuistic Law Governing Primary Rights and Duties," *JBL* 92 (1973): 180-184.

44    Daube, "Biblical Landmarks," 177-180.

revolutionary legislation ... made women equal members of the covenant community."[45]

Daube's argument is narrowly focused; he believes that Deuteronomy for the first time made women who committed adultery legally liable to the community rather than to their husbands. We have set forth and refuted Daube's position in some detail in chapter two.[46]

Phillips argues more broadly that one of the main purposes of the Deuteronomic reformers was to make women "equal members" of the covenant. By "equal members" Phillips means only that women were now "liable for breach of the criminal law."[47]

There is no doubt that the Deuteronomic family laws (and the Deuteronomic laws in general) hold women liable to the laws of the community.[48] The question is whether this is innovative. Were women not liable to the laws of the community prior to the Deuteronomic code?

Phillips' argument appears to have three parts. (1) He holds that women were the property of their fathers or their husbands prior to the Deuteronomic legislation. He bases this in turn on laws in the Book of the Covenant (Ex 21:22; 22:15-16) which assign damages to the husband or father for injuries done to the wife or daughter.[49] (2) Phillips interprets the explicit references to women in the Deuteronomic legislation[50] as an indication that these laws, unlike earlier laws couched in masculine language, made women legally liable.[51] (3) Finally, Phillips points to the adultery laws, especially Deut 22:22, as evidence that the Deuteronomic view of the liability of women was innovative.

We have already argued that women were considered liable to laws against adultery prior to the Deuteronomic legislation. Phillips' view that women were the possessions of their husbands or fathers before but not after the Deuteronomic legislation is also unsustainable. Family laws in both the Book of the Covenant and in Deuteronomy seek to compensate

---

45 Phillips, *AICL*, 16.

46 See pp. 33-35.

47 Phillips, *AICL*, frequently refers to women's full partnership or equal membership in the covenant community. It is only by a careful reading that one discovers that this phrase means only that after the Deuteronomic reform, women were subject to execution if they violated Israel's "criminal law." They "remained entirely under the authority of men .... All the Deuteronomist did was to bring women within the scope of the covenant community, and therefore of the criminal law" (*AICL*, 16).

48 See Deut 22:21, 22, 23-24,; 25:11-12; and, apart from the family laws, Deut 13:7-12; 17:2-7; 22:5; 23:18-19 (Eng 23:17-18).

49 Phillips, *AICL*, 16. Phillips frequently asserts that the Deuteronomic laws changed the legal status of women in Israel. To the best of my knowledge, he does not ever develop that position in an extended or systematic way. My understanding of his argument is based on his discussion at various points in *AICL* and in his commentary.

50 Deut 13:7; 15:12ff.; 17:2-5, etc.

51 Phillips, *Deuteronomy*, 50, 95, 117.

the father or husband of a woman for what modern law would consider an offense against her (Ex 21:22; 22:15-16; Deut 22:19, 29). In neither collection does that mean that the woman was looked on as merely property. It indicates, rather, that the male head of the household controlled that household's finances and that the husband or the father were injured parties.[52]

Nor are the explicit references to women in the Deuteronomic code an indication of its redactors' innovative view of women. The fact that the laws in the Book of the Covenant are couched in masculine language does not mean that those laws would not have applied to women also. Most biblical laws (like most biblical texts) are couched in masculine language. Such language can be used in a gender specific or a generic way. The wording of the laws, therefore, will not often indicate whether they applied to women as well as to men.[53] Deuteronomy's gender specific language may be simply a matter of style.[54]

Finally, Phillips' position is refuted by the presence of two texts which attest to women's liability to the law in predeuteronomic Israel. The Book of the Covenant includes a law prescribing death for a sorceress: מְכַשֵּׁפָה לֹא תְחַיֶּה (Ex 22:17 [Eng. 22:18]). The law probably uses the feminine מְכַשֵּׁפָה, sorceress, because the drafters of the law associated sorcery with women.[55] The story of the ghost wife of Endor (1 Sam 28:8-25) also

---

52  Furthermore, it is unlikely that the damages paid to the father in Ex 22:15-16 or to the husband in Ex 21:22 were looked upon as compensation for injury to the girl. The father of the violated virgin would have been considered an injured party since he now stood to lose her bridewealth. The husband of the woman who miscarried would also be considered an injured party; the fetus was his child.

53  Some Deuteronomic laws include phrases which indicate that they are addressed to a male audience. That cannot be taken automatically as evidence that they were not applied to women. The language of Deut 13:7-12 includes the phrase "if the wife of your bosom," which indicates that it was addressed, in the first place, to men. The wife, however, is clearly liable to the law. She is listed among those who are not to be spared if they conspire to apostasy. Moreover, Deut 23:19 is written in the second person masculine, but it regulates the behavior of a woman: לֹא־תָבִיא אֶתְנַן זוֹנָה ... בֵּית יְהוָה אֱלֹהֶיךָ "You shall not bring a prostitute's wages to the house of Yahweh your God." Who would bring the wages to the temple but the prostitute herself?

54  It is tempting to interpret the explicit references to women in the Deuteronomic laws as evidence that women had acquired more independence since the Book of the Covenant, and thus were more liable to commit offenses.
    The fact that the MAL use gender specific language, however, indicates that such language need not be a sign of women's relatively high or independent status. The MAL presuppose rigidly defined sex roles. The CH, with its higher view of women, is couched in generic language except for those laws which apply only to women. The gender specific language of the MAL may actually be a result of the low status of Assyrian women. Where the two sexes were treated so differently, the drafter of a law who wanted to be clear that it applied to women and to men had to say so explicitly.

55  This is the explanation offered by most commentators. See for example Brevard

provides evidence that women were subject to the law. When Saul, in disguise, asks a ghost wife to conjure up a spirit, she reminds him that Saul has banned such activity. Verse 9 clearly indicates that the woman is afraid of breaking the law: "The woman answered him, 'You know what Saul has done, how he has banned [the use of] ghosts and familiar spirits in the land. So why are you laying a trap for me, to get me killed?'"[56]

These two predeuteronomic texts, then, clearly assume that women are subject to the law.[57] Phillips' position cannot be sustained. The Deuteronomic family laws do not seek to change the legal status of women to "bring them into the covenant" or hold them accountable to the laws of the community. Women had long been liable to the community's laws for many offenses.

## 6. Conclusion

The purpose of the Deuteronomic family laws is neither to promote non-hierarchical relationships between women and men, nor to give women a new legal status. Indeed, the laws are not concerned with women qua women at all. Rather, the purpose of the laws is two-fold. On the one hand, the laws support the order, integrity, and continuity of the family. They do so by undergirding the hierarchical and patrilineal structure of the family. The interests of the family are for the most part identified with the interests of the male. On the other hand, the laws protect the rights of dependent family members. They provide for the social legitimacy and economic security of injured or vulnerable women,

---

Childs, *The Book of Exodus: A Critical Theological Commentary*, Old Testament Library (Philadelphia: Westminster Press, 1974), 477-78; Martin Noth, *Exodus*, Old Testament Library (Philadelphia: Westminster Press, 1962), 185.

56   *Tanakh* (Philadelphia: Jewish Publication Society, 1985).

57   Cuneiform laws and legal documents also indicate that women were subject to the legal processes of the community. Jacobsen, "Ancient Mesopotamian Trial for Homicide," 201, studied 2N-t.54, the trial record and subsequent execution of three men and a woman for the murder of her husband. The trial record (from Nippur and dated from the last half of the eighteenth century B.C.E. during the reign of Rim-Sîn) includes a question "What can a woman do in (such a matter) that she is to be killed?" According to Jacobsen's interpretation, the question is a request to clarify the meaning of "killing." It was assumed that the woman was unlikely to be able to commit the physical act of murder; the question then arose whether an accessory to the act was also subject to capital punishment. What was at stake was not the woman's liability for her action, but the definition of her action. In any case, she was executed.

The MAL (in contrast to the CH) use gender specific language. We therefore know that the laws mandating death for murder (A:10, *ANET*, 181) or the use of magical potents (A:47, *ANET*, 184) apply to women as well as to men. It appears that the MAL give a woman's husband the power to pardon her offenses against him, but not her offenses against anyone else.

and protect dependent family members from false accusation and execution. The legal protection of dependent family members, however, assumes the context of the hierarchically structured family; the laws do not challenge those hierarchical structures in any fundamental way.

# Conclusions

Several recent scholars have argued that the Deuteronomic laws exhibit a "peculiarly humanistic" view of women or a non-hierarchical view of gender relationships within the family. An examination of the presuppositions and purposes of the Deuteronomic family legislation calls into question this assessment of the Deuteronomic view of women.

The Deuteronomic family laws presuppose that women are dependent on their participation in male-headed families for their social and economic well-being. Within the family, the woman's status varies, depending upon her role as mother, daughter or wife. Her status is always viewed as to some degree subordinate to the male head of the household.

In the Deuteronomic view, the woman in her role as mother comes closest to achieving parity with her male counterpart. Offspring owe their mother as well as their father respect and obedience (Deut 21:10-14, 18-21). The mother and father together appear to be responsible for the conduct of their offspring (Deut 21:18-21; 22:13-21). The parity between the mother and the father, however, exists only in their direct relationship to their children. The subordinate role of the mother in the law of the slandered bride (Deut 22:13-21) suggests that the father has priority in a matter related to his offspring if it involves an inter-family dispute. In her role as daughter, the woman's status is similar to the status of the son in that both are subordinate to the parents. Both must obey the parents. Both are valued. The content of their obligations, (visible in the breach) differs, however. The charges against the rebellious son (Deut 21:18-21) include drinking and gluttony, behaviors which make a man a poor leader. The girl is charged with unchastity. Her primary obligation is to preserve her sexuality for her husband; her primary function is to bear and raise his children. Finally, the subordination of the wife to her husband is seen in his economic control of the household, in his unilateral and absolute claim over her sexuality, and in his unilateral power to initiate marriage and divorce.

The laws do not assume that the power and authority of the male head of household is unlimited. Dependent members of the family, including women, are subject to the laws and judicial processes of the community, not to the private justice of the father or husband. They are guarded by protective laws and customary rights. Nonetheless, the laws do assume a hierarchically structured family in which primary authority is vested in the male head of household and which is defined in terms of the man.

The purpose of the Deuteronomic family laws is to ensure the stability of the family. The family structures undergirded by these laws are hierarchical, patrilineal, and patrimonial, however. Bird's statement about biblical law in general aptly describes the Deuteronomic family legislation: "One of the chief aims of Israelite law is to assure the integrity, stability and economic viability of the family as the basic unit of society. In this legislation, however, the interests of the family are commonly identified with those of its male head."[1] Thus we have seen that the Deuteronomic laws seek to undergird the order of the family; they do so by asserting the authority of parents over their offspring and the control of husbands of their wives' sexuality. The laws seek to maintain the integrity of the family by stringently reinforcing male control of women's sexuality. The laws seek to ensure the continuity of the family; this continuity is defined in terms of providing the father with a male heir.

The Deuteronomic family laws do aim at protecting dependent family members, including women. The primary or, more often, secondary aim of several of the laws is to ensure the economic security and social status of injured or vulnerable women. The laws express concern that all persons, including dependent family members, be granted due judicial process. Nonetheless, none of these protective laws challenges that hierarchical, male-defined structure of the family in any fundamental way. Moreover, they presuppose the authority of the male head of the household even as they set limits on that authority.

---

1    Bird, "Images of Women," 51.

# Sources Consulted

Achtemeier, Elizabeth. *Deuteronomy, Jeremiah*. Proclamation Commentaries. Philadelphia: Fortress Press, 1978.

Albright, William F. "The High Place in Ancient Palestine." In *Volume du Congres, Strasbourg, 1956*, by the International Organization for the Study of the Old Testament. Supplements to *Vetus Testamentum*, vol. 4. Leiden: E. J. Brill, 1957.

Alt, Albrecht. "Zu *Hit'ammēr*." *Vetus Testamentum* 2 (1952): 153-159.

Amsler, Samuel. "La Motivation de l'Ethique dans la Parenese du Deuteronome." In *Beiträge zur alttestamentlichen Theologie: Festschrift für Walther Zimmerli*, edited by H. Donner. Goettingen: Vandenhoeck & Ruprecht, 1977.

Andersen, Francis I. "Israel Kinship Terminology and Social Structure." *The Bible Translator* 20 (1969): 29-39.

Anderson, Arnold. "Law in Old Israel: Laws Concerning Adultery." In *Law and Religion: Essays on the Place of the Law in Israel and Early Christianity*, edited by Barnabas Lindars. Cambridge: James Clarke & Co., 1988.

André, G. "*Ṭāmē'*." *Theological Dictionary of the Old Testament*, vol. 5. Grand Rapids: Wm. B. Eerdmans Publishing Co., 1986: 330-342.

Ap-Thomas, D. R. "Some Aspects of the Root *ḤNN* in the Old Testament." *Journal of Semitic Studies* 2 (1957): 128-148.

Baab, O. J. "Father." *The Interpreter's Dictionary of the Bible*, vol. 2. Nashville: Abingdon Press, 1962: 245.

_____. "Family." *The Interpreter's Dictionary of the Bible*, vol. 2. Nashville: Abingdon Press, 1962: 238-241.

_____. "Sex, Sexual Behavior." *The Interpreter's Dictionary of the Bible*, vol. 4. Nashville: Abingdon Press, 1962: 296-301.

_____. "Virgin." *The Interpreter's Dictionary of the Bible*, vol. 4. Nashville: Abingdon Press, 1962: 787-788.

_____. "Widow." *The Interpreter's Dictionary of the Bible*, vol. 4. Nashville: Abingdon Press, 1962: 842-843.

_____. "Woman." *The Interpreter's Dictionary of the Bible*, vol. 4. Nashville: Abingdon Press, 1962: 864-867.

Batto, Bernard Frank. *Studies on Women at Mari*. Baltimore: Johns Hopkins University Press, 1974.

Beattie, Derek Robert George. "The Book of Ruth as Evidence for Israelite Legal Practice." *Vetus Testamentum* 24, 3 (1974): 251-267.

Bellefontaine, Elizabeth. "Deuteronomy 21:18-21: Reviewing the Case of the Rebellious Son." *Journal for the Study of the Old Testament* 13 (1979): 13-31.

Belkin, Samuel. "Levirate and Agnate Marriage in Rabbinic Cognate Literature." *Jewish Quarterly Review* 60 (1969-1970): 275-329.

Benjamin, Don C. *Deuteronomy and City Life: A Form Criticism of Texts with the Word City ('îr) in Deuteronomy 4:41-26:19*. Lanham, Maryland: University Press of America, 1983.

Ben-Barak, Zafrira. "Inheritance by Daughters in the Ancient Near East." *Journal of Semitic Studies* 25 (1980): 22-33.

_____. "The Legal Background to the Restoration of Michal to David." In *Studies in the Historical Books of the Old Testament*, edited by John Adney Emerton. *Supplements to Vetus Testamentum*, vol. 30. Leiden: E. J. Brill, 1979.

Bergman, Jan. "*Bēn*." *Theological Dictionary of the Old Testament*, vol. 2. Grand Rapids: Wm. B. Eerdmans Publishing Co., 1975: 145-159.

Bergman, Jan, et al. "*Bethûlāh.*" *Theological Dictionary of the Old Testament*, vol. 2. Grand Rapids: Wm. B. Eerdmans Publishing Co., 1975: 338-343.

Bigger, Stephen F. "The Family Laws of Leviticus 18 in Their Setting." *Journal of Biblical Literature* 98, 2 (1979): 187-203.

Bird, Phyllis. "Images of Women in the Old Testament." In *Religion and Sexism: Images of Woman in the Jewish and Christian Traditions*, edited by Rosemary Radford Ruether. New York: Simon and Schuster, 1974.

_____. "The Place of Women in the Israelite Cultus." In *Ancient Israelite Religion*, edited by Patrick D. Miller et al. Philadelphia: Fortress Press, 1987.

_____. "'To Play the Harlot': An Inquiry into an Old Testament Metaphor." In *Gender and Difference in Ancient Israel*, edited by Peggy L. Day. Minneapolis: Fortress Press, 1989.

Blenkinsopp, Joseph. "Deuteronomy." In the *New Jerome Bible Commentary*, edited by Raymond Brown. Englewood Cliffs, New Jersey: Prentice Hall, 1990: 94-109.

Boecker, Hans Jochen. *Law and the Administration of Justice in the Old Testament and Ancient East*. Translated by Jeremy Moiser. Minneapolis: Augsburg Publishing House, 1980.

DeBoer, P. A. H. "Some Remarks on Exodus 21:7-11." *Orientalia Neerlandica* (1948): 162-166.

Branson, Robert Dean. "A Study of the Hebrew Term שׂנא." Ph.D. diss., Boston University, 1976.

Braulik, Georg. "Das Deuteronomium und die Menschenrechte." *Theologische Quartelschrift* 166 (1986): 8-24.

_____. "Die Abfolge der Gesetze in Deuteronomium 12-26 und der Dekalog." In *Das Deuteronomium: Entstehung, Gestalt und Botschaft*, edited by Norbert Lohfink. Leuven: University Press, 1985.

_____. "Zur Abfolge der Gesetze in Deuteronomium 16:18-21:23. Weitere Beobachtungen." *Biblica* 69 (1988): 63-92.

Brichto, Herbert C. "Kin, Cult, Land, and Afterlife--A Biblical Complex." *Hebrew Union College Annual* 44 (1973): 1-54.

_____. *The Problem of "Curse" in the Hebrew Bible*. Journal of Biblical Literature Monograph Series, vol. 13. Philadelphia: Society of Biblical Literature and Exegesis, 1963.

Bright, John. *Jeremiah: A New Translation with Introduction and Commentary*. The Anchor Bible. Garden City, N.Y.: Doubleday & Co., 1965.

Brooks, Beatrice Allard. "Some Observations Concerning Ancient Mesopotamian Women." *The American Journal of Semitic Languages and Literatures* 39 (1922-1923): 187-194.

Brown, Francis, S. R. Driver, and Charles Briggs. *A Hebrew and English Lexicon of the Old Testament*. Oxford: Clarendon Press, 1951.

Brown, John Pairman. "The Role of Women and the Treaty in the Ancient World." *Biblische Zeitschrift* 25, 1 (1981): 1-28.

Brueggemann, Walter. *Genesis*. Interpretation: A Bible Commentary for Teaching and Preaching. Atlanta: John Knox Press, 1982.

Brugman, J. *Essays on Oriental Laws of Succession*. Leiden: E. J. Brill, 1969.

Buis, Pierre, and Jacques LeClercq. *Le Deutéronome*. Sources Bibliques. Paris: J. Gabalda, et Cie, 1963.

Buit, M. du. "Quelques Contacts Bibliques dans les Archives Royales de Mari." *Revue Biblique* 66 (1959): 576-581.

Burrows, Millar. "The Ancient Oriental Background of Hebrew Levirate Marriage." *Bulletin of the American School of Oriental Research* 77 (1940): 2-15.

_____. *The Basis of Israelite Marriage*. American Oriental Series, vol. 16. New Haven,

Conn.: American Oriental Society, 1938.

_____. "Levirate Marriage in Israel." *Journal of Biblical Literature* 59, 1 (1940): 23-33.

Buss, Martin J. "The Distinction Between Civil and Criminal Law in Ancient Israel." *Proceedings of the Sixth World Congress of Jewish Studies*, vol. 1. Jerusalem: World Union of Jewish Studies, 1973: 51-61.

Callaway, Phillip B. "Deuteronomy 21:18-21: Proverbial Wisdom and Law." *Journal of Biblical Literature* 103, 3 (1984): 341-352.

Cameron, Averil, and Amelie Kuhrt, eds. *Images of Women in Antiquity*. Detroit: Wayne State University Press, 1983.

Campbell, Edward. *Ruth: A New Translation with Introduction, Notes, and Commentary*. The Anchor Bible. Garden City, N.Y.: Doubleday & Co., 1975.

Cardascia, Guillume. "Droits Cuneiformes et Droit Biblique." *Proceedings of the Sixth World Congress of Jewish Studies*, vol. 1. Jerusalem: World Union of Jewish Studies, 1973: 63-70.

_____. *Les Lois Assyriennes*. Paris: Les Editions du Cerf, 1969.

Carmichael, Calum M. "A Ceremonial Crux: Removing A Man's Sandal as a Female Gesture of Contempt." *Journal of Biblical Literature* 96, 3 (1977): 321-336.

_____. "A Common Element in Five Supposedly Disparate Laws." *Vetus Testamentum 29 (1979): 129-142.*

_____. *The Laws of Deuteronomy*. Ithaca, N.Y.: Cornell University Press, 1974.

Carroll, Robert P. *Jeremiah: A Commentary*. The Old Testament Library. Philadelphia: Westminster Press, 1986.

Cassin, Elena M. *L'adoption a Nuzi*. Paris: Adrien-Maisonneuve, 1938.

_____. "Pouvoirs de la Femme et Structures Familiales." *Revue d'Assyriologie et d'Archéologie Orientale* 63 (1969): 121-148.

_____. *Le Semblable et le Différent*. Paris: Editions La Découverte, 1987.

Cassuto, Umberto. *Biblical and Oriental Studies*. 2 vols. Jerusalem: Magnes Press, 1973-1975.

Cazelles, Henri. "Pureté et Impureté, Ancien Testament." *Dictionnaire de la Bible Supplément*, vol. 9. Paris: Letouzey & Ané, 1979.

Ceresko, Anthony R. "The Function of *Antanaclasis* (mṣ' 'to find'// mṣ' 'to reach, overtake, grasp') in Hebrew Poetry, Especially in the Book of Qoheleth." *Catholic Biblical Quarterly* 44 (1982): 551-569.

Chamberlain, Gary Alan. "Exodus 21-23 and Deuteronomy 12-26: A Form-Critical Study." Ph.D. diss., Boston University, 1977.

Childs, Brevard. *The Book of Exodus: A Critical Theological Commentary*. The Old Testament Library. Philadelphia: Westminster Press, 1974.

Chirichigno, Greg. "A Theological Investigation of Motivation in Old Testament Law." *Journal of the Evangelical Theological Society* 24, 4 (1981): 303-313.

Clements, Ronald E. *God's Chosen People: A Theological Interpretation of the Book of Deuteronomy*. London: SCM Press, 1968.

_____. *Jeremiah*. Interpretation: A Bible Commentary for Teaching and Preaching. Atlanta: John Knox Press, 1988.

Clifford, Richard. *Deuteronomy With an Excursus on Covenant and Law*. Old Testament Message. Wilmington, Delaware: Michael Glazier, 1989.

Coats, George W. "Widow's Rights: A Crux in the Structure of Genesis 38." *Catholic Biblical Quarterly* 34 (1972): 461-466.

Cohen, Yehudi A. "Ends and Means in Political Control: State Organization and the Punishment of Adultery, Incest, and Violation of Celibacy." *American Anthropologist* 71 (1969): 658-687.

Conrad, J., and G. Johannes Botterweck. "*Zāqēn*." *Theological Dictionary of the Old Testament*, vol. 4. Grand Rapids: Wm. B. Eerdmans Publishing Co., 1980:

122-131.

Craigie, Peter C. *The Book of Deuteronomy*. The New International Commentary on the Old Testament. Grand Rapids: Wm. B. Eerdmans Publishing Co., 1976.

Cruesemann, Frank, and Hartwig Thyen. *Als Mann und Frau Geschaffen*. Kennzeichen, bd. 2. Berlin: Burckhardthaus, 1978.

Cruveilhier, P. "Le Lévirat Chez les Hébreux et Chez les Assyriens." *Revue Biblique* 34 (1925): 524-546.

Daube, David. "Biblical Landmarks in the Struggle for Women's Rights." *Juridical Review* 23, 3 (1978): 177-197.

_____. "*Consortium* in Roman and Hebrew Law." *Juridical Review* 62 (1950): 71-91.

_____. "The Culture of Deuteronomy." *ORITA* 3 (1969): 27-52.

_____. *Studies in Biblical Law*. New York: Ktav Publishing House, 1969.

David, Madeleine. "Hit'āmēr (Deuteronomy 21:14; 24:7)." *Vetus Testamentum* 1 (1951): 219-221.

Davies, Eryl W. "Inheritance Rights and the Hebrew Levirate Marriage." Parts 1, 2. *Vetus Testamentum* 31 (1981): 138-144, 257-268.

_____. "The Meaning of *Pî Šenayim* in Deuteronomy 21:17." *Vetus Testamentum* 36, 3 (1986): 341-347.

Day, Peggy L. "From the Child is Born the Woman: The Story of Jephthah's Daughter." In *Gender and Difference in Ancient Israel*, edited by Peggy L. Day. Minneapolis: Fortress Press, 1989.

_____, ed. *Gender and Difference in Ancient Israel*. Minneapolis: Fortress Press, 1989.

Dion, Paul-Eugene. "Tu Feras Disparaitre le Mal du Milieu de Toi." *Revue Biblique* 87 (1980): 321-349.

Doron, Pinchas. "Motive Clauses in the Laws of Deuteronomy: Their Forms, Functions, and Contents." *Hebrew Annual Review* 2 (1978): 61-77.

Douglas, Mary. *Purity and Danger: An Analysis of Concepts of Pollution and Taboo*. New York: Praeger, 1966.

Driver, Godfrey Rolles, and John C. Miles, eds. *The Babylonian Laws*. 2 vols. Oxford: Clarendon Press, 1952.

_____. *The Assyrian Laws*. Oxford: Clarendon Press, 1935.

Driver, Samuel Rolles. *The Book of Genesis*. 12th ed. Westminster Commentaries. London: Methuen & Co., 1954.

_____. *The Book of the Prophet Jeremiah*. London: Hodder and Stoughton, 1906.

_____. *A Critical and Exegetical Commentary on Deuteronomy*. 3d ed. International Critical Commentary. Edinburgh: T. & T. Clark, 1951.

Durand, Jean-Marie, ed. *La Femme dans le Proche-Orient Antique: Compte Rendu de la 33e Rencontre Assyriologique Internationale (Paris, 7-10 Juillet 1986)*. Paris: Editions Recherche sur les Civilisations, 1987.

Eichler, Barry, et al. "Israelite Law." *The Encyclopedia of Religion*, vol. 7. New York: Macmillan Publishing Co., 1987: 466-480.

Eichrodt, Walther. *Ezekiel: A Commentary*. The Old Testament Library. Philadelphia: Westminster Press, 1970.

Eissfeldt, Otto. "*Adhôn*." *Theological Dictionary of the Old Testament*, vol. 1. Grand Rapids: Wm. B. Eerdmans Publishing Co., 1974: 59-72.

Epstein, Louis M. *Marriage Laws in the Bible and the Talmud*. Cambridge, Mass.: Harvard University Press, 1942.

Epzstein, Leon. *Social Justice in the Ancient Near East and the People of the Bible*. Translated by John Bowden. London: SCM Press, 1986.

Erlandsson, Seth. "*Bāghadh*." *Theological Dictionary of the Old Testament*, vol. 1. Grand Rapids: Wm. B. Eerdmans Publishing Co., 1974: 470-473.

_____. "*Zānāh.*" *Theological Dictionary of the Old Testament*, vol. 4. Grand Rapids: Wm. B. Eerdmans Publishing Co., 1980: 99-104.

Eslinger, Lyle. "The Case of an Immodest Lady Wrestler in Deuteronomy 25:11-12." *Vetus Testamentum* 31 (1981): 269-281.

Exum, J. Cheryl. "Promise and Fulfillment: Narrative Art in Judges 13." *Journal of Biblical Literature* 99 (1980): 43-59.

Falk, Zeev Wilhelm. *Hebrew Law in Biblical Times: An Introduction*. Jerusalem: Wahrmann Books, 1964.

_____. "Hebrew Legal Terms: 3." *Journal of Semitic Studies* 14 (1969): 39-44.

Feigin, Samuel I. "The Captives in Cuneiform Inscriptions." *American Journal of Semitic Languages and Literatures* 50 (1933-1934): 217-245; 51 (1934-1935): 22-29.

Fensham, Frank C. "Gen 34 and Mari." *Journal of Northwest Semitic Languages* 4 (1975): 87-90.

Finkelstein, Jacob J. "Ammiṣaduqa's Edict and the Babylonian 'Law Codes.'" *Journal of Cuneiform Studies* 15 (1961): 91-104.

_____. "The Goring Ox: Some Historical Perspectives on Deodands, Forfeitures, Wrongful Death and the Western Notion of Sovereignty." *Temple Law Quarterly* 46, 2 (1973): 169-290.

_____. *The Ox that Gored*. Transactions of the American Philosophical Society, vol. 71, part 2. Philadelphia: The American Philosophical Society, 1981.

_____. "Sex Offenses in Sumerian Laws." *Journal of the American Oriental Society* 86 (1966): 355-372.

Fishbane, Michael. "Biblical Colophons, Textual Criticism and Legal Analogies." *Catholic Biblical Quarterly* 42 (1980): 438-449.

_____. *Biblical Interpretation in Ancient Israel*. Oxford: Clarendon Press, 1985.

_____. "Torah and Tradition." In *Tradition and Theology in the Old Testament*, edited by Douglas A. Knight. Philadelphia: Fortress Press, 1977.

Frick, Frank S. *The City in Ancient Israel*. Dissertation Series (Society of Biblical Literature) no. 36. Missoula, Mont.: Scholars Press, 1977.

Frymer-Kensky, Tikva. "Law and Philosophy: The Case of Sex in the Bible." *Semeia* 45 (1989): 89-102.

_____. "Patriarchal Family Relationships and Near Eastern Law." *Biblical Archaeologist* 44 (1981): 209-214.

_____. "Pollution, Purification, and Purgation in Biblical Israel." In *The Word of the Lord Shall Go Forth: Essays in Honor of David Noel Freedman*, edited by C. Meyers and M. O'Connor. Winona Lake, Ind.: Eisenbrauns, 1983: 399-414.

_____. "The Strange Case of the Suspected Sotah (Numbers 5:11-31)." *Vetus Testamentum* 34 (1984): 11-26.

_____. "The Trial Before God of an Accused Adulteress." *Bible Review* 2, 3 (1986): 46-49.

Gadd, Par C. J. "Tablets from Kirkuk." *Revue d'Assyriologie et d'Archéologie Orientale* 23, 2-4 (1926): 49-161.

Gelb, Ignace J. "Prisoners of War in Early Mesopotamia." *Journal of Near Eastern Studies* 32 (1973): 70-98.

Gemser, B. "The Importance of the Motive Clause in Old Testament Law." In *Congress Volume Copenhagen, 1953*, by the International Organization of Old Testament Scholars. Supplements to *Vetus Testamentum*, vol. 1. Leiden: E. J. Brill, 1953.

Gerstenberger, Erhard. "Covenant and Commandment." *Journal of Biblical Literature* 84 (1965): 38-51.

Gilmer, Harry W. *The If-You Form in Israelite Law*. Dissertation Series (Society of Biblical Literature) no. 15. Missoula, Mont.: Scholars Press, 1975.

Glazier-McDonald, Beth. "Intermarriage, Divorce, and the *Bat-El Nekar*: Insights into

Malachi 2:10-16." *Journal of Biblical Literature* 106 (1987): 603-611.

Goldingay, John. *Theological Diversity and the Authority of the Old Testament*. Grand Rapids: Wm. B. Eerdmans Publishing Co., 1987.

Good, Edwin M. "Capital Punishment and Its Alternatives in Ancient Near Eastern Law." *Stanford Law Review* 19 (May 1967): 947-977.

Gordon, Cyrus H. "Nuzi Tablets Relating to Women." *Analecta Orientalia* 12 (1935): 164-184.

_____. "The Status of Woman Reflected in the Nuzi Tablets." *Zeitschrift für Assyriologie* 43 (1936): 146-169.

Gordis, Robert. "On Adultery in Biblical and Babylonian Law--A Note." *Judaism* 33, 2 (1984): 210-211.

Gray, John. *Joshua, Judges, Ruth*. The New Century Bible Commentary. Grand Rapids: Wm. B. Eerdmans Publishing Co., 1986.

_____. *1 & 2 Kings*. 2d ed. The Old Testament Library. Philadelphia: Westminster Press, 1970.

Greenberg, Moshe. "More Reflections on Biblical Criminal Law." In *Studies in Bible, 1986*, edited by Sara Japhet. Scripta Hierosolymitana 31. Jerusalem: Magnes Press, 1986.

_____. Review of *Ancient Israel's Criminal Law: A New Approach to the Decalogue*, by Anthony Phillips. *Journal of Biblical Literature* 91 (1972): 535-538.

_____. "Some Postulates of Biblical Criminal Law." In *Yehezkel Kaufmann Jubilee Volume: Studies in Bible and Jewish Religion*, edited by Menahem Haran. Jerusalem: Magnes Press, 1960.

Greengus, Samuel. "Law in the OT." *The Interpreter's Dictionary of the Bible*, Supplementary Volume. Nashville: Abingdon Press, 1976: 532-537.

_____. "The Old Babylonian Marriage Contract." *Journal of the American Oriental Society* 89, 3 (1969): 505-532.

_____. "A Textbook Case of Adultery in Ancient Mesopotamia." *Hebrew Union College Annual* 40 (1969): 33-44.

Grosz, Katarzyna. "Some Aspects of the Position of Women in Nuzi." In *Women's Earliest Records: From Ancient Egypt and Western Asia*, edited by Barbara S. Lesko. Atlanta: Scholars Press, 1989.

Hallo, William W. "The Slandered Bride." In *Studies Presented to A. Leo Oppenheim*. Chicago: The Oriental Institute of the University of Chicago, 1964.

Harris, R. "Woman in The ANE." *The Interpreter's Dictionary of the Bible*, Supplementary Volume. Nashville: Abingdon Press, 1976: 960-963.

Havice, Harriet Katherine. "The Concern for the Widow and the Fatherless in the Ancient Near East: A Case Study in Old Testament Ethics." Ph.D. diss., Yale University, 1978.

Henneger, Joseph. "Zum Erstgebornenrect bei den Semites." *Festschrift für W. Caskel*. Leiden: E. J. Brill, 1968.

Henninger, J. "Premier-Nés en ethnologie." *Dictionnaire de la Bible Supplément*, vol. 8. Paris: Letouzey & Ané, 1972.

Hertzberg, Hans Wilhelm. *1 & 2 Samuel: A Commentary*. The Old Testament Library. Philadelphia: Westminster Press, 1964.

Hiebert, Paula S. "'Whence Shall Help Come to Me?' The Biblical Widow." In *Gender and Difference in Ancient Israel*, edited by Peggy L. Day. Minneapolis: Fortress Press, 1989.

Hobbs, T.R. "Jeremiah 3:1-5 and Deuteronomy 24:1-4." In *Jeremiah and Lamentations*, edited by A. S. Peake. The New Century Bible. New York: Oxford University Press, American Branch, 1910.

Hoffner, Harry A. "*Almānāh*." *Theological Dictionary of the Old Testament*, vol. 1. Grand

Rapids: Wm. B. Eerdmans Publishing Co., 1974: 287-291.

Holladay, William Lee. *Jeremiah: A Commentary on the Book of the Prophet Jeremiah*. 2 vols. Hermeneia. Philadelphia: Fortress Press, 1986, 1989.

Hooks, Stephen M. "Sacred Prostitution in Israel and the Ancient Near East." Ph.D. diss., Hebrew Union College, 1985.

Hoppe, Leslie J. "Deuteronomy on Political Power." *Bible Today* 26 (1968): 261-266.

_____. "Elders and Deuteronomy: A Proposal." *Église et Theologie* 14 (1983): 259-272.

Huehnergard, John. "Biblical Notes on Some New Akkadian Texts from Emar (Syria)." *Catholic Biblical Quarterly* 47 (1985): 428-434.

Humbert, Paul. "Le Substantif *to'eba* et le verbe *t'b* dans l'Ancien Testament." *Zeitschrift für die alttestamentliche Wissenschaft* 72 (1960): 217-237.

Jackson, Bernard S. "The Ceremonial and the Judicial: Biblical Law as Sign and Symbol." *Journal for the Study of the Old Testament* 30 (1984): 25-50.

_____. "Introduction." *Jewish Law Annual* 4 (1981): 3-8.

_____. "Reflections on Biblical Criminal Law." In *Essays in Jewish and Comparative Legal History*. Leiden: E. J. Brill, 1975.

Jacobsen, Thorkild. "Primitive Democracy in Ancient Mesopotamia." *Journal of Near Eastern Studies* 2 (1943): 159-172.

_____. "An Ancient Mesopotamian Trial for Homicide." In *Toward the Image of Tammuz and Other Essays on Mesopotamian History and Culture*. Harvard Semitic Series, vol. 21. Cambridge, Mass.: Harvard University Press, 1970.

Japhet, Sara. "The Relationship Between the Legal Corpora in the Pentateuch in Light of Manumission Laws." In *Studies in Bible, 1986*, edited by Sara Japhet. Scripta Hierosolymitana 31. Jerusalem: Magnes Press, 1986.

Jepsen, A. "Amah und Schiphchah." *Vetus Testamentum* 8 (1958): 293-297.

Johnson, Aubrey R. *The One and the Many in the Israelite Conception of God*. 2d ed. Cardiff: University of Wales Press, 1961.

Kaufman, Stephen A. "The Structure of the Deuteronomic Law." *MAARAV* 1/2 (1978-1979): 105-158.

Kautzsch, Emil, ed. *Gesenius' Hebrew Grammar*. 2d English ed. by A. E. Cowley. Oxford: Clarendon Press, 1910.

Kilmer, Anne Draffkorn. "Symbolic Gestures in Akkadian Contracts from Alalakh and Ugarit." *Journal of the American Oriental Society* 94, 2 (1974): 177-183.

Klein, Hans. "Natur und Recht: Israels Umgang mit dem Hochzeitsbrauchtum seiner Umwelt." *Theologische Zeitschrift* 37, 2 (1981): 3-18.

Koch, K. "*Chātā'*." *Theological Dictionary of the Old Testament*, vol. 4. Grand Rapids: Wm. B. Eerdmans Publishing Co., 1980: 309-319.

Kooy, V. H. "First-Born." *The Interpreter's Dictionary of the Bible*, vol. 2. Nashville: Abingdon Press, 1962: 270-272.

Kornfeld, Walter. "L'Adultere dans l'Orient Antique." *Revue Biblique* 57 (1950): 92-109.

Lacheman, Ernest R. "Note on Ruth 4:7-8." *Journal of Biblical Literature* 56 (1937): 53-56.

Landsberger, Benno. "Jungfräulichkeit: Ein Beitrag zum Thema 'Beilager und Eheschliessung.'" In *Symbolae Juridicae et Historicae Martino David Dedicatae*. Leiden: E. J. Brill, 1968: 41-105.

Lemche, N. P. "The 'Hebrew Slave': Comments on the Slave Law Exodus 21:2-11." *Vetus Testamentum* 25 (1975): 129-144.

_____. "The Manumission of Slaves--The Fallow Year--The Sabbatical Year--The Jobel Year." *Vetus Testamentum* 26 (1976): 38-59.

Lesko, Barbara S., ed. *Women's Earliest Records: From Ancient Egypt and Western Asia*. Brown Judaic Series no. 166. Atlanta: Scholars Press, 1989.

Levine, Baruch A., ed. *Leviticus*. The JPS Torah Commentary. Philadelphia: The Jewish

Publication Society, 1989.

Levine, Etan. "On Intra-familial Institutions of the Bible." *Biblica* 57 (1976): 554-559.

L'Hour, Jean. "Les Interdits *To'eba* dans le Deutéronome." *Revue Biblique* 71 (1964): 481-503.

_____. "Une Législation Criminelle dans le Deutéronome." *Biblica* 44 (1963): 1-28.

Lipinski, E. "The Wife's Right to Divorce in the Light of an Ancient Near Eastern Tradition." *Jewish Law Annual* 4 (1981): 9-27.

Locher, Clemens. "Deuteronomium 22:13-21 vom Prozessprotokoll zum Kasuistischen Gesetz." In *Das Deuteronomium: Entstehung, Gestalt und Botschaft*, edited by Norbert Lohfink. Leuven: University Press, 1985.

_____. *Die Ehre Einer Frau im Israel*. Orbis Biblicus et Orientalis, 70. Goettingen: Vandenhoeck & Ruprecht, 1986.

Loewenstamm, Samuel E. *Comparative Studies in Biblical and Ancient Oriental Literatures*. Alter Orient und Altes Testament 204. Neukirchen-Vluyn: Neukirchener Verlag, 1980.

_____. "Law." In *Judges*, vol. 3, edited by Benjamin Mazar. New Jersey: Rutgers University Press, 1971.

Lohfink, Norbert. "Deuteronomy." *The Interpreter's Dictionary of the Bible*, Supplementary Volume. Nashville: Abingdon Press, 1976: 229-232.

_____. "Die Bundesurkunde des Koenigs Josias." *Biblica* 44 (1963): 261-288.

_____. *Great Themes from the Old Testament*. Translated by Ronald Walls. Edinburgh: T. & T. Clark, 1982.

Long, Burke O. "The Stylistic Components of Jeremiah 3:1-5." *Zeitschrift für die alttestamentliche Wissenschaft* 88 (1976): 386-390.

Lorton, David. "The Treatment of Criminals in Ancient Egypt through the New Kingdom." *Journal of the Economic and Social History of the Orient* 20, 1 (1977): 2-64.

McBride, S. Dean, Jr. "The Deuteronomic Name Theology." Ph.D. diss., Harvard University, 1969.

McCarter, P. Kyle, Jr. *1 Samuel: A New Translation with Introduction, Notes, and Commentary*. The Anchor Bible. Garden City, N.Y.: Doubleday & Co., 1980.

_____. *2 Samuel: A New Translation with Introduction, Notes, and Commentary*. The Anchor Bible. Garden City, N.Y.: Doubleday & Co., 1984.

Mace, David R. *Hebrew Marriage: A Sociological Study*. London: Epworth Press, 1953.

McKeating, Henry. "Sanctions Against Adultery in Ancient Israelite Society, with Some Reflections on Methodology in the Study of Old Testament Ethics." *Journal for the Study of the Old Testament* 11 (1979): 57-72.

_____. "A Response to Dr. Phillips by Henry McKeating." *Journal for the Study of the Old Testament* 20 (1981): 25-26.

McKenzie, John L. "The Elders in the Old Testament." *Biblica* 40 (1959): 522-540.

Malul, Meir. *Studies in Mesopotamian Legal Symbolism*. Alter Orient und Altes Testament 221. Neukirchen-Vluyn: Neukirchener Verlag, 1988.

Manor, Dale W. "A Brief History of Levirate Marriage as It Relates to the Bible." *Restoration Quarterly* 27, 3 (1984): 129-142.

Marcus, David. "Juvenile Deliquency [*sic*] in the Bible and the Ancient Near East." *Journal of the Ancient Near Eastern Society* 13 (1981): 31-52.

Martin, James D. "The Forensic Background to Jeremiah 3:1." *Vetus Testamentum* 19 (1969): 82-92.

Mayes, Andrew David Hastings. *Deuteronomy*. The New Century Bible. Grand Rapids: Wm. B. Eerdmans Publishing Co., 1981.

Mendelsohn, Isaac. "On Marriage in Alalakh." In *Essays on Jewish Life and Thought*, edited by J. Blau et al. New York: Columbia University Press, 1959.

_____. "On the Preferential Status of the Eldest Son." *Bulletin of the American Schools of Oriental Research* 156 (December 1959): 38-40.

_____. *Slavery in the Ancient Near East: A Comparative Study of Slavery in Babylonia, Assyria, Syria, and Palestine from the Middle of the Third Millenium to the End of the First Millenium*. New York: Oxford University Press, 1949.

Meyers, Carol. *Discovering Eve: Ancient Israelite Women in Context*. New York: Oxford University Press, 1988.

Milgrom, Jacob. "The Betrothed Slave-girl, Leviticus 19:20-22." *Zeitschrift für die alttestamentliche Wissenschaft* 89 (1977): 43-50.

_____. "The Alleged 'Demythologization and Secularization' in Deuteronomy." Review of *Deuteronomy and the Deuteronomic School*, by Moshe Weinfeld. *Israel Exploration Journal* 23 (1973): 156-161.

_____. "First-born." *The Interpreter's Dictionary of the Bible*, Supplementary Volume. Nashville: Abingdon Press, 1976: 337-338.

Miller, Patrick D. *Deuteronomy*. Interpretation: A Biblical Commentary for Teaching and Preaching. Louisville: John Knox Press, 1990.

de Moor, J. C. "*Ba'al*." *Theological Dictionary of the Old Testament*, vol. 2. Grand Rapids: Wm. B. Eerdmans Publishing Co., 1975: 181-200.

Moran, William L. "The Scandal of the 'Great Sin' at Ugarit." *Journal of Near Eastern Studies* 18 (1959): 280-281.

Morgenstern, Julian. "The Book of the Covenant, Part 2." *Hebrew Union College Annual* 7 (1930): 19-258.

_____. *Rites of Birth, Marriage, Death, and Kindred Occasions Among the Semites*. Cincinnati: Hebrew Union College Press, 1966.

Muffs, Yochanan. *Studies in the Aramaic Legal Papyri from Elephantine*. Studia et Documenta Ad Irua Orientis Antiqui Pertinentia, vol. 8. Leiden: E. J. Brill, 1969.

Muntingh, L. M. "The Social and Legal Status of a Free Ugaritic Female." *Journal of Near Eastern Studies* 26 (1967): 102-112.

Murray, Daniel E. "Ancient Laws on Adultery--A Synopsis." *Journal of Family Law* 1 (1961): 89-104.

Myers, Jacob M. *1 Chronicles: Introduction, Translation, and Notes*. The Anchor Bible. Garden City, N.Y.: Doubleday & Co., 1965.

Nasuti, Harry P. "Identity, Identification, and Imitation: The Narrative Hermeneutics of Biblical Law." *Journal of Law and Religion* 4, 1 (1986): 9-23.

Neudecker, Reinhard. *Fruehrabbinisches Ehescheidungsrecht*. Rome: Biblical Institute Press, 1982.

Neufeld, Ephraim. *Ancient Hebrew Marriage Laws*. London: Longmans, Green & Co., 1944.

_____. *The Hittite Laws*. London: Luzac & Co., 1951.

Neusner, Jacob. *The Idea of Purity in Ancient Judaism*. Leiden: E. J. Brill, 1973.

Nicholson, Ernest W. *The Book of the Prophet Jeremiah: Chapters 1-25*. The Cambridge Bible Commentary. Cambridge: Cambridge University Press, 1973.

Niditch, Susan. "The Wronged Woman Righted: An Analysis of Genesis 38." *Harvard Theological Review* 72 (1979): 143-149.

Noth, Martin. "The Laws in the Pentateuch." In *The Laws in the Pentateuch and Other Studies*. Edinburgh and London: Oliver & Boyd, 1966.

_____. *Exodus*. The Old Testament Library. Philadelphia: Westminster Press, 1962.

_____. *Leviticus: A Commentary*. Rev. ed. The Old Testament Library. Philadelphia: Westminster Press, 1977.

_____. *Die Ursprunge des Alten Israel im Lichte neuer Quellen*. Köln: Westdeutscher Verlag, 1961.

Orlinsky, Harry M. "Virgin." *The Interpreter's Dictionary of the Bible*, Supplementary

Volume. Nashville: Abingdon Press, 1976: 939-940.

Otto, Eckart von. "Zur Stellung der Frau in den aeltesten Rechtstexten des Alten Testamentes (Exodus 20:14; 22:15f.)-- wider die hermeneutische Naivitaet im Umgang mit dem Alten Testament." *Zeitschrift für Evanglelische Ethik* 26 (1982): 279-305.

Patai, Raphael. *Family, Love and the Bible*. London: MacGibbon & Kee, 1960.

Paradise, Jonathan. "A Daughter and Her Father's Property at Nuzi." *Journal of Cuneiform Studies* 32 (1980): 189-207.

Paterson, John. "Divorce and Desertion in the Old Testament." *Journal of Biblical Literature* 51 (1932): 161-170.

Patrick, Dale. *Old Testament Law*. Atlanta: John Knox Press, 1985.

_____. "Casuistic Law Governing Primary Rights and Duties." *Journal of Biblical Literature* 92 (1973): 180-184.

Paul, Shalom M. "Biblical Analogues to Middle Assyrian Laws." In *Religion and Law: Biblical-Judaic and Islamic Perspectives*, edited by E. B. Firmage et al. Winona Lake, Ind.: Eisenbrauns, 1990.

_____. *Studies in the Book of the Covenant in the Light of Cuneiform and Biblical Law*. Leiden: E. J. Brill, 1970.

*Pedersen, Johannes. Israel: Its Life and Culture*. 2 vols. London: Oxford University Press, 1926.

Phillips, Anthony. *Ancient Israel's Criminal Law: A New Approach to the Decalogue*. Oxford: Basil Blackwell, 1970.

_____. "Another Example of Family Law." *Vetus Testamentum* 30 (1980): 240-243.

_____. "Another Look at Adultery." *Journal for the Study of the Old Testament* 20 (1981): 3-25.

_____. *Deuteronomy*. The Cambridge Bible Commentary. Cambridge: Cambridge University Press, 1973.

_____. "The Laws of Slavery: Exodus 21:2-11." *Journal for the Study of the Old Testament* 30 (1984): 51-66.

_____. "*Nebalah*--A Term for Serious Disorderly and Unruly Conduct." *Vetus Testamentum* 25 (1975): 237-242.

_____. "Some Aspects of Family Law in Pre-Exilic Israel." *Vetus Testamentum* 23 (1973): 349-361.

_____. "Uncovering the Father's Skirt." *Vetus Testamentum* 30 (1980): 38-43.

Philo, of Alexandria. *Philo, with an English Translation*, by F. H. Colson, G. H. Whitaker, and J. W. Earp. The Loeb Classical Library, vols. 1-10, 1929-1962.

Pitt-Rivers, Julian. *The Fate of Shechem; or, the Politics of Sex: Essays in the A. 'hropology of the Mediterranean*. Cambridge Studies in Social Anthropolog,, no. 19. Cambridge: Cambridge University Press, 1977.

Porter, Joshua R. *The Extended Family in the Old Testament*. Occasional Papers in Social and Economic Administration 6. London: Edutext Publications, 1967.

Praag, A. van. *Droit Matrimonial Assyro-Babylonien*. Amsterdam· Noord-Hollandsche Uitgervers Maatschappij, 1945.

Prewitt, Terry J. "Kinship Structures and the Genesis Genealogies." *Journal of Near Eastern Studies* 40, 2 (1981): 87-98.

Pritchard, James B., ed. *Ancient Near Eastern Texts Relating to the Old Testament*. 3d ed. Princeton: Princeton University Press, 1969.

Rabinowitz, Jacob J. "The 'Great Sin' in Ancient Egyptian Marriage Contracts." *Journal of Near Eastern Studies* 18 (1959): 73.

Rabuzzi, Kathryn A. "Family." *The Encyclopedia of Religion*, vol. 5. New York: Macmillan Publishing Co., 1987: 276-282.

Rad, Gerhard von. *Deuteronomy: A Commentary*. Translated by Dorothea Barton. The

Old Testament Library. Philadelphia: Westminster Press, 1966.

_____. *Genesis: A Commentary*. Translated by John Marks. The Old Testament Library. Philadelphia: Westminster Press, 1972.

_____. *Studies in Deuteronomy*. Translated by David Stalker. Studies in Biblical Theology no. 9. Chicago: Henry Regnery Co., 1953.

Rattray, Susan. "Marriage Rules, Kinship Terms, and Family Structure in the Bible." In *Society of Biblical Literature 1987 Seminar Papers*, edited by Kent Harold Richards. Atlanta: Scholars Press, 1987.

Reed, William L. "Some Implications of *ḥēn* for Old Testament Religion." *Journal of Biblical Literature* 73 (1954): 36-41.

Rémy, Pierre. "La condition de la femme dans les codes du Proche-Orient ancien et les codes d'Israel." Parts 1, 2. *Sciences Ecclesiastiques* 16 (1964): 107-127, 291-320.

Rennes, Jean. *Le Deutéronome*. Geneva: Editions Labor et Fides, 1967.

Ringgren, Helmer. *"'Abh."* *Theological Dictionary of the Old Testament*, vol. 1. Grand Rapids: Wm. B. Eerdmans Publishing Co., 1974: 1-19.

_____. *"Tāhar."* *Theological Dictionary of the Old Testament*, vol. 5. Grand Rapids: Wm. B. Eerdmans Publishing Co., 1986: 287-296.

Rofé, Alexander. "Family and Sex Laws in Deuteronomy and the Book of the Covenant." *Henoch* 9, 2 (1987): 131-160.

_____. "The Laws of Warfare in the Book of Deuteronomy: Their Origins, Intent, and Positivity." *Journal for the Study of the Old Testament* 32 (1985): 23-44.

Roth, Martha T. "Age at Marriage and the Household: A Study of Neo-Babylonian and Neo-Assyrian Forms." *Comparative Studies in Society and History* 29 (1987): 715-747.

_____. *Babylonian Marriage Agreements 7th - 3rd Centuries B.C.* Alter Orient und Altes Testament 222. Neukirchen-Vluyn: Neukirchener Verlag, 1989.

_____. "'She Will Die By the Iron Dagger': Adultery and Neo-Babylonian Marriage." *Journal of the Economic and Social History of the Orient* 31 (1988): 186-206.

Rowley, Harold H. "The Marriage of Ruth." In *The Servant of the Lord and Other Essays on the Old Testament*. Oxford: Basil Blackwell, 1952.

Sakenfeld, Katharine Doob. "In the Wilderness, Awaiting the Land: The Daughters of Zelophehad and Feminist Interpretation." *The Princeton Seminary Bulletin* 9, 3 (1988): 179-196.

Saporetti, Claudio. *The Status of Women in the Middle Assyrian Period.* Translated by Beatrice Boltze-Jordan. Monographs on the Ancient Near East, vol. 2. Malibu, Calif.: Undena, 1979.

Schulz, Hermann. *Das Todesrecht im Alten Testament: Studien z. Rechtsform d. Mot - Jumat - Satze*. Beihefte zur Zeitschrift für die alttestamentliche Wissenschaft, vol. 14. Berlin: Verlag Alfred Toepelmann, 1969.

Seibert, Ilse. *Women in the Ancient Near East*. Translated by Marianne Jerzfeld and revised by George A. Shepperson. New York: Abner Schram, 1974.

Shrager, Miriam Y. "A Unique Bibical Law." *Dor le Dor* 15 (1986-1987): 190-194.

Smith, George Adam. *The Book of Deuteronomy*. The Cambridge Bible for Schools and Colleges. Cambridge: Cambridge University Press, 1950.

Snaith, Norman H. *Leviticus and Numbers*. The Century Bible. New ed. London: Thomas Nelson & Sons, 1967.

Snijders, L.A. *"Zûr/Zār."* *Theological Dictionary of the Old Testament*, vol. 4. Grand Rapids: Wm. B. Eerdmans Publishing Co., 1980: 52-58.

Sonsino, Rifat. "Characteristics of Biblical Law." *Judaism* 33 (1984): 202-209.

_____. *Motive Clauses in Hebrew Law: Biblical Forms and Near Eastern Parallels*. Chico, Calif.: Scholars Press, 1980.

Speiser, Ephraim A. *Genesis: Introduction, Translation, and Notes*. The Anchor Bible.

Garden City, N.Y.: Doubleday & Co., 1964.

_____. "Of Shoes and Shekels: 1 Samuel 12:3; 13:21." *Bulletin of the American Society for Oriental Research* 77 (1940): 15-20.

_____. "'People' and 'Nation' of Israel." *Journal of Biblical Literature* 79 (1960): 157-163.

_____. "A Significant New Will from Nuzi." *Journal of Cunieform Studies* 17 (1963): 65-71.

Stager, Lawrence. "The Archaeology of the Family in Ancient Israel." *Bulletin of the American Schools of Oriental Research* 260 (1985): 1-35.

Stähli, Hans-Peter. *Knabe-Jüngling-Knecht: Untersuchungen zum Begriff im Alten Testament.* Frankfurt am Main: Peter Lang, 1978.

*Stamm, Johann J., with M. E. Andrew. The Ten Commandments in Recent Research.* Naperville, Ill.: Alec R. Allenson, 1967.

Steinberg, Naomi. "Adam's and Eve's Daughters Are Many." Ph.D. diss., Columbia University, 1984.

Taber, C. R. "Kinship and Family." *The Interpreter's Dictionary of the Bible*, Supplementary Volume. Nashville: Abingdon Press, 1976: 519-524.

_____. "Marriage." *The Interpreter's Dictionary of the Bible*, Supplementary Volume. Nashville: Abingdon Press, 1976: 573-576.

_____. "Sex, Sexual Behavior." *The Interpreter's Dictionary of the Bible*, Supplementary Volume. Nashville: Abingdon Press, 1976: 817-820.

Thompson, Thomas, and Dorothy Thompson. "Some Legal Problems in the Book of Ruth." *Vetus Testamentum* 18 (1968): 79-99.

Toeg, A. "Does Deuteronomy 24:1-4 Incorporate a General Law on Divorce?" *Dine Israel* 2 (1970): 5-24.

Torrey, Charles C. *The Second Isaiah*. New York: Charles Scribners, 1928.

Tosato, Angelo. "L'onore di una donna in Israele." *Biblica* 68 (1987): 268-276. Translated by Andrea Sterk.

Trible, Phyllis. "Woman in the OT." *The Interpreter's Dictionary of the Bible*, Supplementary Volume. Nashville: Abingdon Press, 1976: 963-966.

Tsevat, Matitiahu. "*Bekhôr.*" *Theological Dictionary of the Old Testament*, vol. 2. Grand Rapids: Wm. B. Eerdmans Publishing Co., 1975: 121-127.

_____. "*Bĕtûlāh.*" *Theological Dictionary of the Old Testament*, vol. 2. Grand Rapids: Wm. B. Eerdmans Publishing Co., 1975: 338-343.

_____. "Marriage and Monarchical Legitimacy in Ugarit and Israel." *Journal of Semitic Studies* 3 (1958): 237-243.

Uitti, R. W. "The Motive Clause in Old Testament Law." Ph.D. diss., Lutheran School of Theology, 1973.

Vaux, Roland de. *Ancient Israel: Its Life and Institutions*. Translated by John McHugh. New York: McGraw-Hill, 1961.

Watson, Paul. "A Note on the 'Double Portion' of Deuteronomy 21:17 and 2 Kings 2:9." *Restoration Quarterly* 8 (1965): 70-75.

Weinfeld, Moshe. *Deuteronomy and the Deuteronomic School*. Oxford: Clarendon Press, 1972.

_____. "Deuteronomy--the Present State of Inquiry." *Journal of Biblical Literature* 86 (1967): 249-262.

_____. "On 'Demythologization and Secularization' in Deuteronomy." *Israel Exploration Journal* 23, 3 (1973): 230-233.

_____. "The Origin of the Humanism in Deuteronomy." *Journal of Biblical Literature* 80 (1961): 241-247.

Weiss, David. "A Note on אשר לא ארשה." *Journal of Biblical Literature* 81 (1962): 67-69.

Wenham, Gordon J. "*Bĕtûlāh* 'A Girl of Marriageable Age.'" *Vetus Testamentum* 22

(1972): 326-348.

_____. *The Book of Leviticus*. New International Commentary on the Bible. Grand Rapids: Wm. B. Eerdmans Publishing Co., 1979.

_____. "The Restoration of Marriage Reconsidered." *Journal of Jewish Studies* 30 (1979): 36-40.

_____. "Why Does Sexual Intercourse Defile (Leviticus 15:18)?" *Zeitschrift für die alttestamentliche Wissenschaft* 95 (1983): 432-434.

Wenham, Gordon J., and J.G. McConville. "Drafting Techniques in Some Deuteronomic Laws." *Vetus Testamentum* 30 (1980): 248-252.

Westbrook, Raymond. "Biblical and Cuneiform Law Codes." *Revue Biblique* 92, 2 (1985): 247-264.

_____. "The Law of the Biblical Levirate." *Revue Internationale des Droits de l'Antiquité* 24 (1977): 65-87.

_____. "Lex Talionis and Exodus 21:22-25." *Revue Biblique* 93, 1 (1986): 52-69.

_____. "Old Babylonian Marriage Law." 2 vols. Ph.D. diss., Yale University, 1982.

_____. "The Prohibition of Restoration of Marriage in Deuteronomy 24:1-4." In *Studies in Bible, 1986*, edited by Sara Japhet. Scripta Hierosolymitana 31. Jerusalem: Magnes Press, 1986.

_____. *Studies in Biblical and Cuneiform Law*. Cahiers de la Revue Biblique, 26. Paris: J. Gabalda et Cie, 1988.

Westermann, Claus. *Genesis: A Commentary*. Translated by John J. Scullion. 3 vols. Minneapolis: Augsburg Publishing House, 1984-1986.

Wilson, Robert R. "Enforcing the Covenant: The Mechanisms of Judicial Authority in Early Israel." In *The Quest for the Kingdom of God: Studies in Honor of George E. Mendenhall*, edited by H. B. Huffmon et al. Winona Lake, Ind.: Eisenbrauns, 1983.

Winter, Urs. *Frau und Goettin*. Goettingen: Vandenhoeck & Ruprecht, 1983.

Wolff, Hans Walter. *Anthropology of the Old Testament*. Philadelphia: Fortress Press, 1974.

Wright, Christopher J. "The Israelite Household and the Decalogue: The Social Background and Significance of Some Commandments." *Tyndale Bulletin* 30 (1979): 101-124.

_____. "What Happened Every Seven Years in Israel?" *The Evangelical Quarterly* 56, 3 (1984): 129-138.

Wright, G. Ernest. "Introduction and Exegesis." *The Book of Deuteronomy*. The Interpreter's Bible, vol. 2. Nashville: Abingdon Press, 1953: 311-537.

Yaron, Reuven. *Introduction to the Law of the Aramaic Papyri*. Oxford: Clarendon Press, 1961.

_____. "On Divorce in Old Testament Times." *Revue Internationale des droits de l'Antiquité* 4 (1957): 117-128.

_____. *The Laws of Eshnunna*. 2d rev. ed. Jerusalem: Magnes Press, 1988.

_____. "The Restoration of Marriage." *Journal of Jewish Studies* 17 (1966): 1-11.

Zakovitch, Yair. "The Woman's Rights in the Biblical Law of Divorce." *Jewish Law Annual 4 (1981): 28-46.*

Zimmerli, Walther. *Ezekiel: A Commentary on the Book of the Prophet Ezekiel*. 2 vols. Translated by James D. Martin. Hermeneia. Philadelphia: Fortress Press, 1979.

# TRE

## Theologische Realenzyklopädie

### Studienausgabe, Part 1

**Volumes 1 (Aaron) — 17 (Katechismuspredigt)
and complete index**

In cooperation with *Horst Robert Balz, James K. Cameron, Wilfried Härle,
Stuart G. Hall, Brian L. Hebblethwaite, Richard Hentschke, Wolfgang Janke,
Hans-Joachim Klimkeit, Joachim Mehlhausen, Knut Schäferdiek, Henning Schröer,
Gottfried Seebaß, Clemens Thoma*

Edited by *Gerhard Müller*

**1993. 13.5 × 20.5 cm. 17 vols. and index vol. Approx. 800 pages per vol.
Paperbound DM 1.200,−; US $795.00    ISBN 3-11-013898-0**

In 1976, **Walter de Gruyter** began publishing the *Theologische Realenzyklopädie*
(TRE), an essential reference work on theological research being conducted around the
world. We are now pleased to announce the publication of a *paperbound Studienausgabe, at a price substantially lower than the hardcover edition.* The first 17 volumes
are now available. In aproximately seven to eight years, the next set of volumes continuing the **Studienausgabe** will be published. The additional volumes that will complete the set will be offered at a later date.

The TRE resumes and continues the 3rd edition of the *Realencyklopädie für die protest-
antische Theologie und Kirche* (RE[3]), which ended with the 24th volume in 1913. Since
that time, there has been no other comprehensive compilation of theological research
on the scale of the TRE. The radical changes in theory and practice, in terms of contents
as well as methodology, that have taken place in the last decades have necessitated the
publication of such a thorough and complete compendium of theological knowledge.

In the more than 3,000 key word entries, contemporary exegetical, historical, dogmatic,
ethical, and practical theological research are given articulate expression. Philosophy,
history of religions, and Judaic studies are integrated into the presentation when they
contribute to the understanding of the history and present state of Christianity. All of
these disciplines are represented by an international group of editors, thereby eliminat-
ing denominational and national biases.

*Prices subject to change.*

Walter de Gruyter          Berlin · New York

# Christianity and Modern Politics

Edited by
Louisa S. Hulett

1993. Large-octavo. IX, 453 pages.
Cloth ISBN 3-11-013462-4
Paperback ISBN 3-11-013461-6

Anthology of writings on Religion and Politics in the United States of America.

*Sample contents:* Definitions of Christianity, Civil Religion, and Politics · Separation of Church and State in America · Religious Freedom and the Supreme Court · The Rise of Christian Fundamentalism · Fundamentalism versus Secular Humanism · Just War Doctrine · Pacifism and Nuclear Ethics · Liberation Theology.

---

Margaret Ann Palliser, O. P.

# Christ, Our Mother of Mercy

Divine Mercy and Compassion in the Theology
of the *Shewings* of Julian of Norwich

1992. Large-Octavo. XIV, 262 pages. Cloth
ISBN 3-11-013558-2

Julian's image of Christ as the compassionate "mother" of mercy represents her mature theological vision of divine mercy. Julian's trinitarian theology, christology, soteriology, and anthropology are explored within the framework of her understanding of the relationship between kind (nature), mercy and grace. This study includes exhaustive references to the Middle English text of the *Shewings*, bibliography and index.

---

Walter de Gruyter      Berlin · New York